"This book take[s us on a journey]
exploring the sto[ries of Biblical women,]
faith-based truth[s ...] ...ght provoking, and it is
and journal guid[e ...]
impossible to follow Coote's process and not walk away knowing
yourself and your marriage a little better."

Katrina D Hamel, author of *Dividing Sword,* founder of Jump in the Way

"I am always looking for ways to work on myself and my marriage. It wasn't long before I stumbled upon the encouraging words of the humble writer Aminata in her book, "Through God's Eyes: Marriage Lessons for Women." I felt so fulfilled and motivated to push on in polishing my character as I strive to be the best wife God has blessed me to be. My wish is that you purchase this book. Treasures await you as you interactively learn about the marriage lessons for women. Happy reading!"

Carl-Ann, newlywed reader

"... a really riveting read. Practical and relevant message for both males and females. Biblical without being overly theological. A must-read for the married and those hoping to get married."

Marie, Church and Pastors Council member

"In a culture that looks to Hollywood for romantic inspiration and marital advice, Ami Coote's book Through God's Eyes: Marriage Lessons for Women is like a breath of fresh air. Ami is a skilled storyteller with a creative way of keeping your attention from start to finish. I read through the book in one sitting but it would be a great devotional for wives looking to intentionally invest in a Christian marriage. The way Ami brought each marriage from Scripture to life and gave practical application for a 21st-century God-girl was inspiring. This is a must read for any wife looking to grow her marriage and see it through God's eyes."

Tiffany Montgomery, founder of Hope Joy in Christ

"Getting married for women is perhaps the ultimate form of affirmation. You are loved, you are seen, you've been chosen. What could possibly go wrong? Well, as it turns out, lots. *Through God's Eyes: Marriage Lessons for Women* is one woman's heartfelt generosity poured out on all of us. Aminata teaches, mentors, advises and corrects, all while making you chuckle to yourself.

This book is rich, filled with Biblical history, Scriptures and wisdom. Reading the lessons and doing the journaling is like participating in an intensive workshop where Biblical women are your facilitators, drawn together in one place, just to instruct and motivate you. It is steeped in practical honesty and the spirit of sisterhood. Aminata wants us all to have excellent marriages, she yearns for it, and that's as clear and crisp in her writing as it would be if she were having weekly coffee with us. These lessons are timeless, and even after my own fifteen years of marriage I found new and invigorating hope in this book."

Latasha Strachan, founder of Caribbean Women of Faith (formerly The Journey)

"I am totally smitten with Aminata's way of breaking up large marriage issues into bite-sized pieces, and I especially like how she has journal prompts at the end of each section. It really makes it feel less daunting, particularly when working through a personal and current marriage issue. Each chapter is like a mini-sermon, with several biblical references to help draw out the meaning. Her ability to draw context clues and actually use previous verses for additional context really brings this marriage study up a notch. I have a really hard time with studies that look at one passage as the "proof" of meaning, and then they move on. Aminata does not do that; she instead draws on additional biblical AND historical context to discuss a particular meaning. Great format and easy to follow—but the prompts aren't always easy which is great!"

Ashley Spang, motherhood lifestyle blogger at GrowingSpangs.com

"Through God's Eyes: Marriage Lessons for Women as a must-read for women who want to be godly wives. The comparison and co-relation with women and wives in the Bible are on point and helps put into perspective what we experience in a relationship and how God wants us to behave. I also recommend this book for men. It is a good resource for the husband who wants to walk in the glory of God and who wishes to better understand, treat and appreciate their wives for who they are. This book helps us as men to take a look at how a woman thinks, feels and perceives (we get to see marriage through their eyes). Our wives are a part of us, and we must treasure them (1 Peter 3:7).

This book is a great, short read—read it together or in your own private time where both spouses can gain something so they can better love each other and get closer to the mind of God on his intentions and expectations for marriage."

Abraham Lindo, happily married for over ten years to his first and only girlfriend

THROUGH GOD'S EYES:
Marriage Lessons for Women

Also by Aminata Coote

How to Find Your Gratitude Attitude

THROUGH GOD'S EYES:
Marriage Lessons for Women

AMINATA COOTE

Copyright © 2019 by Aminata Coote

All rights reserved. No part of this publication may be reproduced, distributed, or transmitted in any form or by any means, including photocopying, recording, or other electronic or mechanical methods, without the prior written permission of the publisher, except in the case of brief quotations embodied in critical reviews and certain other noncommercial uses permitted by copyright law. For permission requests: Aminata@hebrews12endurance.com.

Names: Coote, Aminata
Title: Through God's Eyes: Marriage Lessons for Women
Identifiers: ASIN: B07MVP66DT | ISBN: 9781724035790 (pbk.)
Subjects: Marriage—Religious aspects—Christianity

Unless otherwise stated, Bible verses quoted in this book are taken from the NKJV Bible.
Scripture taken from the New King James Version®. Copyright © 1982 by Thomas Nelson. Used by permission. All rights reserved.

THE HOLY BIBLE, NEW INTERNATIONAL VERSION®, NIV® Copyright © 1973, 1978, 1984, 2011 by Biblica, Inc. ® Used by permission. All rights reserved worldwide.

Scripture quotations marked (NLT) are taken from the Holy Bible, New Living Translation, copyright © 1996, 2004, 2007, 2013, 2015 by Tyndale House Foundation. Used by permission of Tyndale House Publishers, Inc., Carol Stream, Illinois 60188. All rights reserved.

Scriptures marked KJV are taken from the KING JAMES VERSION (KJV): KING JAMES VERSION, public domain.

Emphases in Scripture quotations are added by the author.

Cover design by Marco Coote & Aminata Coote
Image courtesy of Canva.com

Dear reader, this book is for you. It stands as a testament that the word of God is living and active and has the power to change your life.

Contents

Acknowledgments xi
Introduction xiii
Match Made in Heaven 17
Trouble in Paradise 29
Leave & Cleave 41
No Longer My Girl 43
Through Thick and Thin 55
High School Sweethearts 63
When the Storms Come 77
Stolen Moments 83
Is There Grace in Your Marriage? 95
This Is Not a Hollywood Marriage 97
Miracles Happen 111
The Ten Commandments of Marriage 117
Looks Can Be Deceiving 121
Who Do You Love? 131

Contents

The Wise Woman & Her Foolish Husband 141

What Am I Worth? 151

The Love Verses Check-Up 163

For the Love of a Mother-in-Law 167

A Love Like This 179

For Want of a Good Wife 189

Is the Fruit of the Spirit Evident in Your Marriage? 197

Wrong Kind of Girl 201

When Love Turns to Hate 213

Embracing Your Identity as the Proverbs 31 Woman . 225

Notes 231

About the Author 235

Acknowledgments

I want to say thanks to my Heavenly Father who gave me the opportunity to write this book. He brought me on such a long complicated journey to get to this place that to tell would fill the pages of another book.

Marco and Dominic, thank you for your willingness to support me. I'm grateful that you're running this race with me.

To my street team—Marie, Deidre, Carl-Ann—your input was invaluable. Thank you.

To my launch team—I couldn't have done this without you.

Katrina, your feedback on formatting was spot on. Thank you so much.

Denise, my very vocal cheerleader, I appreciated all the calls you made to check on the progress of this book.

Introduction

I'm told girls dream of marriage; that they plan their wedding and playact it many times. That was never my reality. I didn't dream much about Prince Charming but I knew he was rich, handsome, and willing to grant my every desire. And, of course, we were madly in love—what we would do after the first rush of love was never defined.

Instead, I devoured countless books and dreamed about traveling to far away places and living an exotic life. I read about Egypt and riding on camels. I lived in small towns and big cities as a dancer, librarian, actress... it all depended on the reality the author created for me.

My ideas about love came from books—Sweet Dreams, Sweet Valley High, Mills and Boon, and Harlequin books. The hero and heroine were always well-suited to each other. Their love was strong enough to overcome all challenges. What little conflict they experienced was resolved before the end of the book.

Fast-forward a few years when I became the second half of a relationship. To my surprise, my partner did not know what I was thinking. He was thoughtless more times than not. I didn't miraculously change into a sweet and perfect bride. We argued and our conflict wasn't always resolved in a jiffy.

As I matured, I realized life was a lot different than fiction. While girls grow up on romance novels and movies, boys grow up on video games, action films and the need to appear macho before their friends. There was a complete disconnect.

Was it just me though? Am I the only person who realized those fairy-tale endings don't happen in real life? I couldn't understand why the guy didn't show up when I decided I was ready for a relationship. And when the guy did show up—he wasn't the Prince Charming I was expecting. My husband is wonderful but he's a man with flaws.

In ways, he seems to have different expectations for our relationship than I do. It can be challenging because neither of us can understand why the other isn't acting as expected. These disjointed expectations cause discord between us.

 I still consider myself a bit of a reluctant wife. I chafe at things like obedience and submission. I become slightly resentful because the bulk of the housework falls on me whether I have a full-time job or not. I am not Betty Homemaker. I resent anyone who suggests that's who I need to be to earn the title "Perfect Wife and Mother". I am a woman with flaws. Together my husband and I are learning to balance our expectations with the realities of marriage.

 You may wonder what made me an expert in marriage. I'm not. I don't have a degree in psychology or 20-something years of coaching married couples. I'm just a girl who once spent 31 days examining what the Bible had to say about marriage and learned a whole lot of things. These things have increased as I now look at these teachings in the Bible in a new way. I'm no longer taking the stories at face value. I'm trying to understand what it meant then, so I can figure out how it applies to me now. I want to show you some of those things I learned in the hopes you will apply them to your marriage. We will get some marriage advice from the best resource in the world: the Bible.

 As we walk through this book, we're going to see some of the mistakes which can happen in a marriage. We're also going to see what marriage should look like through God's eyes. This book explores seventeen couples from the Bible. I need you to commit to walking through the lessons from these couples with me.

Introduction

Grab your Bible and get ready to dig deeper into these familiar stories. Keep a journal and a pen handy to write down your observations and the lessons God reveals to you.

Are you ready? Let's go.

Aminata

One

Match Made in Heaven

Once upon a time, there was a beautiful garden. There were flowers of different shapes and sizes. The varied hues of color made it seem as if you were walking in a rainbow.

In this garden lived a man named Adam. He was very happy. He had more food than he could ever eat in his lifetime and a job he loved. He had a lot of animals and the Best Friend in the whole world.

But each day when his friend went home, Adam was by himself. As beautiful as his home was, he was lonely. He noticed all the animals came in pairs: male and female. There wasn't anyone who seemed like a match for him. He was different. And in his difference, he became lonesome.

Seeing how lonely he was, his best friend decided to find a match for him. He created the perfect woman for Adam.

It was love at first sight. They committed their lives to each other in a simple and intimate garden ceremony. Everything was perfect—
Until after the honeymoon.

The fact that you're reading this book leads me to believe you're married. Congratulations. Welcome to the oldest and most distinguished institution in the world. Because you're reading this book, I know you have questions. Maybe you're wondering what happens next. You met the guy. Fell in love. Had the wedding of your dreams (hopefully) and thought life would be like a fairytale. Only it wasn't. Now that you have to live with him, you realize you don't know your spouse quite as well as you thought.

The fairytales didn't tell us cute, little quirks can become annoying. Romance books don't tell you sometimes living with your great love will feel like having a roommate. We couldn't have known our Pookie-bear could ever do anything to make us angry. Oh my darling, it's just the beginning. The sooner you accept that his quirks are permanent, the easier it will be to move on to more important things.

Things like understanding what God wants us to learn from the Bible about marriage. That's an important task—one which will help us to become better wives and, better role models to our children. Our sons will learn from us what to expect from and look for in the women they marry. Our daughters will learn to be women of high moral standards. They may even learn to be, gasp, the Proverbs 31 woman.

THE MAN WAS A WHOLE AND COMPLETE PERSON

✢ Read Genesis 2:8–25

There are many lessons to learn from this passage. Popular culture teaches that each person needs their other or better half for them to be complete. This creates in us a mindset that we need someone to complete us as if we were somehow incomplete. But God did not create any incomplete beings. He created male and female—independent of each other—to crave connection with Him.

The first thing we notice in Genesis 2 is that the man had a relationship with his Heavenly Father and a job. The media teaches us many things. It tells us a woman is independent and does not need anyone to take care of her. It teaches us we don't need anyone—not even God. There is a belief in some sectors we are our own gods.

I wanted to start here because there's a very real lure between the good girl and the bad boy. This tension appears often in romantic literature. Because of it, most of us girls grow up thinking if a bad boy loved us, really loved us, we could reform him. This isn't true. Unless someone wants to change for themselves—their own personal reasons—the change won't stick. They will keep going back to their bad habits as a dog goes back to his own vomit.

I put that there on purpose. I want the image to be stuck in your head so you remember you can't change a man. Neither can your husband force you to change the things you're unwilling to change. You're not looking for a "good guy" either. You want a man who is in an intimate, passionate relationship with his Heavenly Father. That's the man who will love you and cherish you; the man your Heavenly Father wants you to partner with.

Now, let's talk about the whole job thing. Life's hard and unemployment happens. But if a man leans into unemployment, avoid him. It's important for a man to work, even more so than for a woman. "For shame," you're probably thinking. "The International Association of Bra-Wearing Women should confiscate all your bras and burn them."

Yes, well, I used to consider myself a feminist too, and then I read the Bible. God met me on the pages and taught me a few things. A woman was created to be an ezer. She was made to be man's companion. Immediately after creating man, God put him to work as a gardener and caretaker. This desire to work and tend things is ingrained in men. That's a good thing.

There are a whole plethora of young men in my country who don't work. They leave school and start to "hustle"—which is sometimes a fancy word for begging and cheating people. Societies are overrun with gangs whose members are almost exclusively young men who don't work. There's a new breed of men who believe it is a woman's responsibility to take care of them.

This does not mean if your husband falls into hard times and loses his job you should leave him. After all, you did promise "for better or worse, for richer or poorer". What I am suggesting is you should choose a partner who knows God and who believes a man should work—one who seeks to be employed at all times.

My pastor puts it this way: an unemployed man should be a miserable man because he knows he is the main provider for his family.

WOMAN WAS CREATED TO BE MAN'S HELPER

And the Lord God said, "It is not good that man should be alone; I will make him a helper comparable to him" (Genesis 2:18).

I remember reading this verse in high school. I had become angry because I thought God created women to be men's helpers—as in their maids. I had good reason to think this was the case. As an eighties child, I grew up hearing many girls are inferior to boys sentiments. Of course, that's not what the Bible meant. Let's look at this verse through God's eyes:

The word translated as help or helper in the verse is the Hebrew word ezer[1]. Ezer comes from the root word azar which means to surround, that is, protect or aid, succor.

The word ezer appears twenty-one times in the Old Testament[1].

Let's look at a few of them.

I will lift up my eyes to the hills—
From whence comes my help?
My help comes from the Lord,
Who made heaven and earth. Psalm 121:1-2

You who fear the Lord, trust in the Lord;
He is their help and their shield. Psalm 115:11

"O Israel, you are destroyed,
But your help is from Me." Hosea 13:9

The word help in those verses, (I've underlined them for you) is the English translation for ezer. Here's the best thing: did you notice these texts are talking about God? If God calls Himself an ezer it must be a great thing to be.

The New International Version renders Genesis 2:18 this way:

The LORD God said, "It is not good for the man to be alone. I will make a helper suitable for him."

Before God created woman, He wanted to make sure she would be a suitable ezer.

When something is suitable, it is considered appropriate for a specific person, purpose, or situation. God wanted man's partner to be acceptable, satisfactory, custom-made, well qualified, well suited, competent, capable, right, appropriate, desirable, and ideal.

I've included all the references to ezer below so you can look them up in your Bible. I wrote the word ezer in mine every time it appears, so when I read those verses I can remember what an ezer is. This is optional for you, but I hope you will look up the passages and make a note of what you think it means to be an ezer. Go ahead, I'll wait.

- Genesis 2:18
- Genesis 2:20
- Exodus 18:4
- Deuteronomy 33:7
- Deuteronomy 33: 26
- Deuteronomy 33: 29
- Psalm 20:2
- Psalm 33:20
- Psalm 70:5
- Psalm 89:19
- Psalm 115:9–11
- Psalm 121:1–2
- Psalm 124:8
- Psalm 146:5
- Isaiah 30:5
- Ezekiel 12:14
- Daniel 11:34

Now we understand being an ezer is not about being a maid. An ezer is a companion, defender, and protector all rolled into one. We get a better idea of what God intended when He created the first couple. Both of them had equal responsibility for tending the garden. Both had dominion over the other created things (Genesis 1:26–28).

GOD KNEW MAN WAS LONELY BEFORE HE DID

↳ Read Genesis 1:26–27, 2:18–20

"God said, "Let Us make man in Our image, according to Our likeness" (Genesis 1:26).

What does it mean to be made in the image of God? Some believe it has to do with our physical makeup: two eyes, two ears, a torso, legs and so forth. This belief gets very confusing when we try to envision God as a being who can be everywhere at once. Our limited human understanding cannot fully conceptualize what God is like. For our purposes, to be made in the image of God means we have similar attributes. Some of God's attributes are:

Characteristics that are to be retained, sought after.

- **Love:** 1 John 4:8, John 15:13, Psalm 136:26
- **Justice:** Isaiah 61:8, Deuteronomy 32:4, 1 Peter 1:17
- **Holiness:** Leviticus 19:19, 1 Peter 1:15–16, 1 Samuel 2:2
- **Mercy:** Psalm 145:9, Ephesians 2:4–5, Lamentations 3:22–23
- **Protector and defender:** 2 Samuel 22:3–4, 2 Thessalonians 3:3, Psalm 32:7
- **Capacity to hate:** Proverbs 6:16–19, Psalm 11:5, Romans 9:13

In Exodus 34:6–7, God says this about Himself:
"The Lord, the Lord God, merciful and gracious, longsuffering, and abounding in goodness and truth, keeping mercy for thousands, forgiving iniquity and transgression and sin, by no means clearing the guilty, visiting the iniquity of the fathers upon the children and the children's children to the third and the fourth generation."

As people created in God's image, we have the capability to reflect all these attributes in our lives. God, who created us because He loved us (Ephesians 1:4), made mankind with the ability to love.

It was no surprise to God that man was lonely. It had always been God's intention to make male and female. That's why He said, "Let us give them dominion" (Genesis 1:27).

Before Adam realized he was the only one of his kind, God stated it was not a good thing for him to be alone. Why then did God not immediately remedy the situation?

Let's reread Genesis 2:18–20:

And the Lord God said, "It is not good that man should be alone; I will make him a helper comparable to him." Out of the ground the Lord God formed every beast of the field and every bird of the air, and brought them to Adam to see what he would call them. And whatever Adam called each living creature that was its name. So Adam gave names to all cattle, to the birds of the air, and to every beast of the field. But for Adam there was not found a helper comparable to him.

We recognize from Genesis 1:24–27 that God created animals before Adam. After making the observation that it was not good for man to be alone, God brought all the animals to Adam for him to name. I can imagine the animal parade lasted a very long time. During this process, Adam realized all the animals came in pairs. There were a male and a female version of every creature. Maybe he wondered why, or he asked God for the reason. More importantly, Adam realized there was no female version of himself.

I believe God wanted Adam to desire companionship from someone who was the female counterpart of himself.

When we look at the creation of woman this way, we appreciate that we were created to fill a need man had—not a need to cook, iron and clean—a need for companionship. It makes sense God would create an ezer who could play all those roles in the life of man.

Through God's eyes, the wife had a vital role. She was a desirable addition to the earthly family.

THE EXPECTATION OF INTIMACY

When God decided to make woman by taking a rib out of the side of man, He made a deliberate choice. He could have followed the same steps He had when He made Adam.

And the Lord God formed man of the dust of the ground, and breathed into his nostrils the breath of life; and man became a living being (Genesis 2:7).

Eve could have been formed from the dust of the earth out of original material but that's not what happened. God took a rib from man's side and used it to create his ezer (Genesis 2:21–22). You may have heard Matthew Henry's famous quote:

"The woman was made of a rib out of the side of Adam; not made out of his head to rule over him, nor out of his feet to be trampled upon by him, but out of his side to be equal with him, under his arm to be protected, and near his heart to be beloved."

I'll put it another way, God wanted the woman and the man to have an intimate connection. He wanted them to be a part of each other. The bond between a man and his wife should be similar to the bond between parents and their children.

The husband ought to be aware of how his actions affect his wife. The wife needs to understand how her actions affect her husband. This completely shatters the belief that each of us is independent. Yet, if we are to have the kind of marriage God intends, we need to learn this key truth.

"And they were both naked, the man and his wife, and were not ashamed" (Genesis 2:25). Intimacy is an integral part of any marriage. If one person shares everything and there is no reciprocation, the other person will shut down and eventually close off their heart. Women tend to be more vocal than men. We have an intrinsic desire to talk about stuff. You may need to encourage your husband, especially in those early years, to share things with you.

Make sure you are communicating the important things with him. It is imperative for him to share the significant things with you. For every couple, that's going to look a bit different, so the two of you need to figure out what your big things are. Some typical big things are:

- How will you spend your income?
- Where will you live?
- What are your beliefs about child rearing?
- Where will you go to church?

- What are the responsibilities each person has?
- How will you spend your days off?
- What do you have in common and what are your differences?
- When you have an argument, how will you resolve them?
- What does intimacy look like for you?

I did say intimacy was a big deal, right? That's why God says, "a man shall leave his father and mother and be joined to his wife, and they shall become one flesh" (Genesis 2:24). If you love hugs and kisses but your hubby thinks grunting at you is affection—you will have a challenge. Both of you need to get together early in your marriage and figure out what your big things are.

Journal

Make a note of you and your husband consider big things in your journal and refer to them periodically. Be sure to update this list as what you consider a big thing will change as you do.

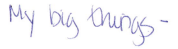

Two

Trouble in Paradise

One day, after they had been married for some time, the woman found herself some distance from her husband. While standing by herself, she was approached by a serpent. The serpent struck up a conversation with her. In a very short time, he had Eve questioning things she had taken for granted.

He was cunning. He painted a picture of excitement and danger. He made her want something she knew she shouldn't have. Because she had drifted from her husband, she couldn't ask for his advice and so she did a foolish thing.

It didn't end there. She got her husband involved and soon they were in trouble. Their best friend was hurt and the relationship changed forever. They lost their home, their friends, their job. Their entire lifestyle had to change. Nothing would ever be the same again.

We started off by looking at the only example of a perfect marriage so we have an idea of what God had intended. Unfortunately for us, what began as perfect did not remain that way.

All the examples going forward are going to be after sin had entered the world so don't be surprised if it reads like a soap opera or at least a very dramatic show. The characters in the Bible were real people. They experienced fear, pain, doubt, and love as we do.

CONTROL THE DRIFT

↪ Read Genesis 3:1–20

There are two schools of thought among Bible scholars when discussing the temptation of Eve and the fall of mankind. Traditional Jewish interpretation and commentator John Milton believe Adam was standing beside Eve when the serpent tempted her. However, commentators Matthew Poole and Joseph Benson believe the two had been in separate locations[1].

I fall into the second school of thought because I find it hard to believe Adam would have stood silently while the serpent misquoted him and God. I prefer to think Adam was busy working in another part of the garden when Eve wandered away. That's the framework we're going to use to discuss this passage.

Adam was preoccupied and Eve drifted away from him.

Remember how we talked about the importance of intimacy in your marriage? Well, let's talk about it some more. Intimacy is the close bond you feel with someone. The person makes you comfortable and you are familiar with them. In the context of a marriage, this means both parties feel comfortable with each other. The two are generally on the same wavelength.

We don't know why Eve wandered away from Adam, but when one partner wanders from the other, it's never a good thing. It's imperative both persons take the whole "cleaving together thing" as a big deal.

The word translated as cleave in the King James Version of the Bible is the Hebrew dabaq[2] which could also translate:

To cling, keep close, abide fast, follow close (hard after), be joined (together), keep fast, pursue hard.

Isn't that an awesome picture? When God said:

Therefore shall a man leave his father and his mother, and shall cleave unto his wife: and they shall be one flesh in Genesis 2:24, He was saying:

Therefore shall a man leave his father and his mother, and shall cling to, keep close to, abide fast with, follow close to (hard after), be joined (together) with, keep fast to, pursue hard his wife and they shall be one flesh.

If we hold on to our spouses and they hold on to us, the divorce statistic would not be as high as it is today[3]. I'm not going to repeat them here because I'm sure you've heard them many times.

When used figuratively, dabaq means to catch by pursuit. I like to think this means a husband is always pursuing his wife. He doesn't allow the relationship to get stale. He continues to court her long after the memories of the wedding begin to fade—until death do they part. Wouldn't that be nice? Don't you want to be pursued by your Mister? Especially on those days when you feel frumpy and out of sorts?

As your hubby chases you, pursue him—seeking after him passionately every day of your lives together—as eagerly as you did when you were dating. The two of you should be partners. Partners who work together. Learn together. Grow together. Communicate with each other. When we don't practice intimacy, we drift apart. Unless we control our natural ability to drift, we won't remain intimate with the person we chose to do life with.

Journal

Make note of those areas you and partner are perfectly in sync. Write another list of the ways you differ (for example, preferences, hobbies, outlooks, character traits, etc.).

The areas where you don't share the same perspective are the ones which have the greatest possibility to drive you apart. We have to be vigilant in guarding our intimacy. We have no idea why Eve wasn't by Adam's side, but our lesson from her is to remain conscious of our spouses. We need to make an effort to stay connected with our partner as we have to make an effort to stay connected to God.

BE CAREFUL WHO YOU LET INFLUENCE YOU

Did you realize how little effort it seemed to take for Satan to have Eve question God? Peer pressure is a real thing—even for us big girls. For that reason, it's important for us to surround ourselves with people who have a similar mindset. As women who follow a holy God, we have to associate with people who not only know God is holy but want to be like Him. The truth about influence is we underestimate its effects until we see the results it has had on us.

Let's take an active look at this. In your journal, write a list of some of the characteristics of a friend.

The following Bible verses show us what friendship looks like through God's eyes.

A friend loves at all times. Proverbs 17:17

As iron sharpens iron, so a man sharpens the countenance of his friend Proverbs 27:17

The righteous should choose his friends carefully, for the way of the wicked leads them astray. Proverbs 12:26

Do not be deceived: "Evil company corrupts good habits." 1 Corinthians 15:33

How will you know if someone loves you? The answer is found in 1 Corinthians 13:4–8:

Love suffers long and is kind; love does not envy; love does not parade itself, is not puffed up; does not behave rudely, does not seek its own, is not provoked, thinks no evil; does not rejoice in iniquity, but rejoices in the truth; bears all things, believes all things, hopes all things, endures all things.
Love never fails.

If someone loves you, they will always be kind. It does not mean they won't tell you tough truths, it means when they do, they have your best interest in mind. A person who loves you shows it in tangible and intangible ways, you won't have to wonder, you'll know.

When something bad happens, your friend won't rejoice while you suffer. If you're in trouble and your friends start gloating, you may need to think about parting ways.

One of the best examples of biblical friendship is David and Jonathan. We can read a great synopsis of their relationship in 1 Samuel 20. Jonathan was loyal to David though it meant he would not inherit the throne. He stood with David against Saul, his father, though it almost cost him his life.

Do you have a friend like that in your life? Are you a friend like that to someone? Do you and your spouse provide that kind of friendship for each other?

A man who has friends must show himself friendly (Proverbs 18:24). Good friends give us words to encourage and strengthen instead of words which tear us down.

KNOW WHAT YOU BELIEVE AND WHY

Do you have principles and values that guide your life? Of course, you do. You may not have thought about it before, but you deal with things in a consistent manner. And, there are things you would never consider doing, no matter the circumstances. Your principles determine the way you behave in particular situations. Our principles are expressed by our actions.

Values are harder to define, at least, according to the dictionary. Our values are the reasons we behave in a particular way. What are the things you consider important? What drives you? Our values are found in our motives.

Journal

List your current values. Write a code of conduct which explains how your values affect the way you do things.

What are some of the things that were important to you six months ago? One year ago? Five years ago? Are they still important now? Why or why not?

Note: Values change as we do. Something you hold valuable today may not be as important in five years or in a month. As our values change, it is necessary for us to update our code of conduct.

Do you have a good handle on what your values and principles are? Good. Why do you have them? Why do you believe the things you believe? Is it because of your parents? Your friends? Your spouse? Did something happen in your past to impact the way you behave? We need to know what we believe and why we believe them.

✤ Read Genesis 39:1–10

In this passage, we meet Joseph who is a slave in Potiphar's household. In Genesis 39:6, we learn Potiphar had "left all that he had in Joseph's hand". A few verses later, we find the missus trying to get the young man to sleep with her. His response to her was:

"Look, my master does not know what is with me in the house, and he has committed all that he has to my hand. There is no one greater in this house than I, nor has he kept back anything from me but you, because you are his wife. How then can I do this great wickedness, and sin against God?" (Genesis 39:8-9)

Joseph wasn't told: "You have access to everything except my wife." It was Joseph's principles which caused him to interpret the instructions in that manner. A less principled man than Joseph would have jumped at the opportunity to have sex with Mrs.

Potiphar. He would have interpreted Potiphar's instructions as permission.

If you keep reading, you'll see Joseph thrown into prison for not sleeping with his master's wife. Wait, what? Do you mean staying true to my values can get me in trouble? Yes, sometimes. That's why you have to understand why they are your values in the first place. In Joseph's case, he knew if he slept with Mrs. Potiphar, he committed a sin against God. The physical consequences he suffered for staying true to his principles were immaterial. Joseph knew he was accountable to a Higher Authority.

If Eve had known why she believed touching the fruit would kill her, maybe she would not have been deceived. It's essential for us to have a reason for our particular values. We may be asked to defend them to someone, maybe even to ourselves.

THE DESIRE TO BE LIKE GOD

"For God knows that in the day you eat of it your eyes will be opened, and you will be like God, knowing good and evil" (Genesis 3:5). After Satan made this statement, Eve considered the possibilities:

- She inferred that the fruit was edible.
- The fruit was beautiful to look at.
- Eating it would make her as wise as God.

This desire to be like God remains in our nature and can be either good or bad. As humans, we were created to have a connection with our Heavenly Father. We forge connections through intimacy. Intimacy grows as our knowledge of the person increases. We can know who God is by studying His attributes as revealed in nature and in Scripture. As we learn more about God, we begin to trust Him and long to become more like Him.

God has two types of attributes: communicable and incommunicable. God's communicable attributes are things we can reflect and adapt. His incommunicable attributes are exclusive to Him. Jen Wilkin wrote this about God in her book In His Image:

"Only God is infinite, incomprehensible, self-existent, eternal, immutable, omnipresent, omniscient, omnipotent, and sovereign. When we strive to become like him in any of these traits, we set ourselves up as his rival. Human beings created to *bear the image* of God aspire instead to *become like* God. We reach for those attributes that are only true of God, those suited only to a limitless being[4]".

That's why aspiring to be like God can either be a bad or a good thing. If our desire is to reflect the character of God, wonderful. We are called to model the behavior of Jesus who is the author and finisher of our faith. When we insist on pursuing things God says we should not have, we set ourselves above Him. We become a sort of idol to ourselves.

Eve sought to be sâkal. The Hebrew word sâkal[5] means: to be or act circumspectly and hence, intelligent, deal prudently. Her desire for prudence caused her to act unwisely. As wives, we have to be careful we don't make the same mistake Eve did. Was it wrong of Eve to desire wisdom? No, but the wisdom that comes from this earth is not the kind God wants us to have.

James tells us if any man wants wisdom he should ask God. He goes on to say the wisdom that comes from God is pure, while earthly wisdom is "demonic and sensual" (James 1:5, 3:15–17).

Journal

What things are you craving that are not God's will for you? Why do you think God doesn't want you to have them?

Pray and ask God to forgive you for wanting things outside of His will for you. Ask Him to remove the desire for that particular thing from you.

Pause to Reflect

Leave & Cleave

For this cause shall a man leave his father and mother, and shall cleave to his wife, and the two shall become one flesh. Ephesians 5:31 KJV

When we follow this simple concept, it has a profound impact on our marriages. Husbands should leave their parents and cleave to their wives. If the husband is leaving and cleaving, the wife should do the same.

In a nutshell:

Leaving involves accepting our responsibilities. Many marriages would have been saved but for the fact that Mummy and Daddy were waiting in the wings to rescue "their baby" from their big, bad husband or wife. Barring cases of abuse or neglect, parents should allow their adult offsprings the chance of a successful marriage. A marriage won't work if one or both parties believe that at the first sign of trouble they'll go home.

Raise your hand if your mother-in-law thinks no woman on earth is perfect for her little boy. Or, if your parents don't think any man on earth is good enough for their little princess.

Leaving means we leave childish thinking and behavior behind. (At least, we make a serious attempt to try.)

Cleaving involves creating a new life and an intimate relationship with your spouse. This is the person who's going to be with you through the trials of life—parenting, sickness, health, the death of a loved one, tight finances, natural disaster, stress at work, emotional turmoil, spiritual growth, spiritual stagnancy—you name it and your partner will be there for it. This person is your cheerleader, counselor, friend, priest, prayer partner, masseuse and the list goes on.

Cleaving refers to the bond the two should share. The two form a new entity, one that cannot be easily broken.

Journal

What does leaving and cleaving mean to you?

Three

No Longer My Girl

Once upon a time, there was a great feast in the land. The king had invited all the nobles and officials in the kingdom to celebrate with him. This wasn't any ordinary feast—it was 180 days of celebrating his splendor.

At the end of those six months, there was to be another feast in Shusan. There would be a week-long celebration in the king's garden. Gold and silver couches filled the hall of the palace. Couches sat on a mosaic pavement of alabaster, turquoise, and white and black marble. Drinks were served in golden vessels each of which was an original. There was royal wine in abundance and every man could drink as much, or as little, as he wanted.

It was a time of great jubilee for every man, woman, and child in the citadel of Shusan as the queen was also having a feast and everyone was invited.

WIVES SHOULD SUBMIT

➔ Read Esther 1

This chapter causes controversy for the modern woman. How dare King Ahasuerus request that Queen Vashti appear before him and his drunken friends? I wouldn't have gone either. I'm not a piece of chattel to be paraded around like a piece of ... oh dear—

Before we go off on a female rant, let's backtrack a bit. Do you remember when God told Eve that her desire would be to her husband? No?

Let's reread Genesis 3:16b:

"Your desire shall be for your husband,
And he shall rule over you."

The word translated as desire is the Hebrew tshuwqah[1]. Tshuwqah also means stretching out after; a longing: desire.

Tshuwqah occurs three times in the Old Testament[1]. Let's dig into them to see if we can get a better understanding of the phrase "Your desire shall be for your husband".

"If you do well, will you not be accepted? And if you do not do well, sin lies at the door. And its desire is for you, but you should rule over it" (Genesis 4:7).

Hmm, if we use the extended definition of the Hebrew word tshuwqah we get this:

"If you do well, will you not be accepted? And if you do not do well, sin lies at the door. And its desire (stretching out after; longing: desire) is for you, but you should rule over it."

This verse was God's response to Cain after refusing his unacceptable sacrifice. The Heavenly Father was telling His son that sin was stretching after him. Sin consumes whatever it touches and the result is destruction and death.

I am my beloved's,

And his desire (stretching out after; longing: desire) is toward me (Songs of Solomon 7:10).

This was Solomon's beloved's response to his impassioned speech about how much he desired her—in food terms:

"Your navel is a rounded goblet."

"Your waist is a heap of wheat."

"Your stature is like a palm tree and your breasts are like coconuts."

Err, you get the point. Why don't you and the Mister schedule some time to read Songs of Solomon together? The passion found there may surprise you.

Your desire (stretching out after; longing: desire) shall be for your husband,

And he shall rule over you (Genesis 3:16b).

If we're stretching after or longing for our husbands, does that mean we lust after them? Or does it mean we want his place of dominance in the family? The text points to the second response being more likely.

God included the caveat "and he shall rule over you" for a purpose. It was about the distribution of power. Otherwise, male and female would have continued to have equal dominance.

The word translated rule in the English Bible is the Hebrew word mâshal[2]. Mâshal also means to rule: (have, make to have) dominion, governor, reign, (bear, cause to, have) rule, ruling, ruler, have power.

Mâshal is pronounced maw-shal—does that sound like a familiar English word? It's looking more like we're going to be fighting for dominance, doesn't it?

Back to our passage:

In his intoxicated state, King Ahasuerus wanted to display his invaluable possession: Vashti. He sent seven eunuchs to bring her to the ball to show off her crown and her beauty. She refused.

According to Oriental tradition, males and females did not intermingle in society[3]. If Queen Vashti had appeared before the men, she would have been breaking this tradition. Does this mean Vashti had no choice but to refuse?

Ephesians 5:22–24 reads:

Wives, **submit to your own husbands**, as to the Lord. For the husband is head of the wife, as also Christ is head of the church; and He is the Savior of the body. Therefore, just as the church is subject to Christ, so **let the wives be to their own husbands in everything** (emphasis added).

I have bolded the parts I want us to focus on. As wives, we have a duty to submit—yes, I know submit is a dirty word—but we have to. It's what God requires.

The original Greek word for submit is hypotássō[4]. Alternate meanings are to subordinate; to obey, be under obedience, put under, subdue unto, put in subjection to/under, submit self unto.

Hypotássō appears 49 times in the New Testament. Here are a few examples (the corresponding translation is underlined):

And he went down with them, and came to Nazareth, and was <u>subject</u> unto them: but his mother kept all these sayings in her heart. Luke 2:51 KJV

And the seventy returned again with joy, saying, Lord, even the devils are <u>subject</u> unto us through thy name. Luke 10:17 KJV

For he hath <u>put</u> all things under his feet. But when he saith all things are <u>put under</u> him, it is manifest that he is excepted, which did <u>put</u> all things <u>under</u> him. 1 Corinthians 15:27 KJV

Who shall change our vile body, that it may be fashioned like unto his glorious body, according to the working whereby he is able even to <u>subdue</u> all things unto himself. Philippians 3:21 KJV

<u>Submit yourselves</u> therefore to God. Resist the devil, and he will flee from you. James 4:7 KJV

When you submit, you accept or yield to the authority or will of another person.

A cursory look at these verses reveals that change happens after submission. If we are to get the marriage we desire, we need to exhibit the behavior God commands.

As God-girls, we have to get to the place where we desire to follow the Lord with all our heart, soul, mind and strength. When we get to that place of ultimate commitment, submission won't feel like walking into a den of hungry lions. Instead, it will be something we desire and choose to do.

The Bible says a lot more about how wives are to conduct themselves. The texts below show us how marriage looks through God's eyes.

- Proverbs 31:10–31
- Colossians 3:18
- Hebrews 13:4–7
- I Corinthians 7:1–16

Use them to review your own actions against the standard set by God. In your journal, make a note of how well you submit to your husband. Please don't use this as an opportunity to criticize yourself. Instead, see it as an opportunity to bring your shortcomings to God in prayer. Ask Him to fill the gaps in your service as a wife.

BE CONSCIOUS OF THE EXAMPLE YOU SET

The king and his officials were angry at Vashti's response because of the impact it would have had on the nation. Imagine it:

The women were having a wonderful time. There was more food than some of them had seen in a lifetime and more drink than they could handle. There was music and dancing; best of all, the queen was there. She was the most beautiful woman in the world and they were in the same room with her. Queen Vashti was telling a funny story when there was a knock at the door. One of the maids answered it. Standing in the doorway were King Ahasuerus' seven eunuchs.

"A message for the queen." one of them shouted.

"Yes, what is it?" The Queen's maid answered. She inclined her neck and looked down her nose at him.

"The king is requesting Her Honor's presence in the main hall." said another.

"She is to come wearing the royal crown." decreed a third.

Queen Vashti's upper lip tightened. She straightened her spine and clutched the arms of her throne. Whispers fluttered through the hall.

"How rude."

"The nerve of that man."

"How dare he summon her like that?"

All eyes turn to Queen Vashti. What would she do? Everyone waited for her response.

"I will not go." She tilted her chin as she said the words.

"But the king—" sputtered the eunuchs in chorus.

"I have spoken." replied the queen with a wave of her hand. "Dismissed."

She turned her head and continued her story as if nothing had happened. There was a shocked silence before the audience of women once again erupted into whispers.

"Did you see what the queen did?"

Meanwhile, the seven men stood outside the door, uncertain. What should they do? She was the queen—they couldn't force her to appear before the King. Could they? The King would be furious. Would he believe them when they told him his wife had refused to come?

Shoulders slumped, they returned to the hall where the rowdiness had gotten louder. All the men waited for the appearance of the queen, some of them had never seen her before. Legend had it that she was the most beautiful woman in the kingdom. The door opened, and all eyes zoomed in on the seven eunuchs.

The seven eunuchs shuffled across the hall and pretended all the men weren't staring at them. They stood beside the King. The bravest eunuch leaned towards him.

"She will not come," he whispered.

"What do you mean she will not come?" boomed the king. The musicians' fumbled and the dancing stumbled to a halt. All activity stopped.

The queen had refused an audience with the king. All eyes were on the throne as they waited to see and hear what the King would do.

Everyone in the fortress of Shushan was at one of the two week-long feasts. All eyes were on Vashti. All eyes were on Ahasuerus. Without realizing it, Vashti was on the verge of setting a trend of disobedience among wives. If not for the advice the king had received, the Women's Liberation Movement would have begun that night.

Sometimes like Vashti, we are not aware of the way we are influencing those around us. We may not be aware of those who observe our actions and mimic our behavior. As God-girls, we have to remember that when nobody else sees us, God does. Are we being good witnesses for Him?

Journal

Think for a moment of the influence you currently hold: are you setting a good example? If you had a daughter or a young mentee, how would you want to influence them to be good wives? How would you encourage them to walk as daughters of the King?

Write down the lessons you would want to impart. How are you doing? Are you walking according to your ideal standard?

TWO WRONGS DON'T MAKE A RIGHT

→ Read Esther 1:10–12

Did Vashti have a right to refuse the king's request? She didn't have to appear before a roomful of drunken men, did she?

There are two people at fault here. King Ahasuerus' actions contradicted the principle found in Ephesians 5:25–29. He wasn't "cherishing her as if she were his own body". He belittled Vashti's position as queen by treating her as another possession. He showed neither love nor respect for her.

Queen Vashti had received a direct order from her husband, the king. Both his title and his relationship to her were reasons for her to be obedient. In other words, she should have obeyed him because he was her king, and, because he was her husband. Vashti did not follow the principle of submission found in Ephesians 5:22–24.

In our marriages, there are going to be cases where there is fault on both sides. Each party can continue to accuse the other of wrongdoing, or one person can choose to take the high road. Yes, I'm asking you to take the path of humility.

In a situation where the two of you are wrong, apologize for the error that you made and agree to disagree. The sooner we settle these disagreements in our marriages, the healthier they will be. Intimacy is important, remember? Well, you can't be intimate with someone if you're mad at them. Besides, everyone knows after a fight you get to make up. Won't that be fun?

Four

Through Thick and Thin

Once there was a lonely, young lady. Her name was Hagar. She was far away from her home and was living in a foreign land, among strange people. These persons spoke, ate, and worshipped differently. She wondered if things would ever get any easier.

One day, the mistress of the house where she was living asked her for a huge favor. The mistress wanted Hagar to be the surrogate mother to her children as she was unable to have any of her own. It sounded unusual, but she agreed. There was a catch: Hagar would have to sleep with the man of the house.

"I'm okay with it." The Mistress assured her. *"My husband is on board too, he thinks you're very pretty. You would be his second wife."*

The Master had great wealth and was well-respected by his peers. As his second wife, her status within the household would improve. She would no longer be a slave. Of course, she'd do it.

Everything was fine until Hagar got pregnant. Then, if truth be told, she had become boastful. She wanted the Mistress to realize she was the one having a baby. It would be her child.

DON'T INVITE OTHER PEOPLE INTO YOUR MARRIAGE

✧ Read Genesis 16

At the time this event occurred, polygamy was an accepted cultural practice. It was not unusual for men to have multiple wives, especially when the primary wife was barren.

Genesis 16 recounts the tale of Abraham, Sarah, and Hagar—a love triangle. There's a lot we can learn from this trio about what not to do in a relationship, so let's get started.

Honey, there are going to be times when that man drives you nuts. He will leave the dirty dishes in the sink. He will put his dirty clothes everywhere except in the hamper. He will sometimes ignore you in favor of his beloved hobby, but—

You have to handle these moments with care. Yes, you may want to vent to your best friend, your mother or whoever, and you have some leeway to do that, but do it carefully. What do I mean by that?

There are going to be a lot of persons who are important to you and will be privy to the details of your life. We're human. Because we were created to be social beings, we will talk about our personal lives. However, you have to remember people will see your hubby through your eyes. They are going to imagine him based on what you say about him and not on his character.

Have you ever heard horrible things about someone, only to meet them and had to wonder if it was a different person you had heard about? The same thing can happen when you speak negative things about your spouse. Let's face it: we talk a lot of junk when we're mad. We say things we don't mean or things that are untrue.

When we are venting about the latest eye-rolling thing our spouse did, we have to be mindful of our tone. Remember those people who are watching and mimicking our behavior when we aren't aware? They're present in these situations too.

Don't only talk about the things you're mad about, talk about the things he does well. Did he cook dinner last week? Talk about that. Did he rub your feet after a bad day at work? Tell *that* story.

Another reason for being careful what we say about our spouse is that we don't know who is listening. Not every person who sits beside us nodding their heads at our tirade is with us. There are some manipulative people in this world. Do you want to give someone ammunition to destroy your marriage? Then watch your tongue. Proverbs 14:1 teaches that the wise woman builds her house, but the foolish pulls it down with her hands. It's your job to guard the intimacy and integrity of your marriage. Don't be a foolish woman.

WHEN HE DOES AS YOU ASK, DON'T GET MAD

Have you ever asked your boo to do something and he did exactly as you asked? But, because you didn't like the result, you got mad? Or you never thought he would do it, so when he did ... I know. Me too.

This is what happened with Abraham and Sarah. She thought she could control the situation. She believed she could choose the perfect surrogate mother to have a perfect son, and things would be, well, perfect. I imagine her looking at all the women she knew trying to decide who would be the best fit.

She may have looked at the width of their hips, the way their features fit together. The other woman had to be pretty—not so pretty that she would outshine her—but pretty enough to attract Abraham. Maybe she imagined what the child would look like. Or, she chose a woman that had similar features to herself. Either way, when the situation spiraled out of her control, she got mad.

Then Sarai said to Abram, "My wrong be upon you! I gave my maid into your embrace; and when she saw that she had conceived, I became despised in her eyes. The LORD judge between you and me" (Genesis 16:5).

The word translated as wrong in the New King James Version is the Hebrew word châmâç[1]. Châmâç could be translated as violence, cruel, cruelty, damage, or injustice.

According to the Strong's Concordance, there are 60 occurrences of the Hebrew word châmâç in the King James Bible[1]. We'll look at a few of them to get a better idea of the context (the corresponding translation is underlined).

The earth also was corrupt before God, and the earth was filled with <u>violence</u>. Genesis 6:11

That the <u>crime</u> done to the seventy sons of Jerubbaal might be settled and their blood be laid on Abimelech their brother, who killed them, and on the men of Shechem, who aided him in the killing of his brothers. Judges 9:24

Do not envy the <u>oppressor</u>,
And choose none of his ways. Proverbs 3:31

Let the <u>violence</u> done to me and my flesh be upon Babylon,"
The inhabitant of Zion will say;
"And my blood be upon the inhabitants of Chaldea!"
Jerusalem will say Jeremiah 51:35

The context of Genesis 16:5 shows Sarah blaming Abraham for the way Hagar treated her. How was it Abraham's fault? It had been Sarah's idea. Abraham had done exactly as she had asked him. But because the result wasn't quite what she was expecting, she blamed him. I love the way the New Living Translation Bible renders this verse:

"Then Sarai said to Abram, 'This is all your fault! I put my servant into your arms, but now that she's pregnant she treats me with contempt. The LORD will show who's wrong—you or me!'" (Genesis 16:5 NLT)

Let's not be Sarah. When our hubby listens to us and does as we ask, let us give him credit for that, regardless of the outcome.

GOD DOESN'T NEED OUR HELP

Isn't it interesting how Sarah could ask God to judge the situation after things had gone bad? Why hadn't she asked for His help before she had implemented her solution?

There are going to be times in our marriages when we feel that we have to fix things. I believe that women have a "fixer" gene. (This is not the fixer-upper gene that makes your husband do household repairs). Women like things to be neat and nice and in their proper place. And that can cause us to be impatient sometimes. Impatience can lead to recklessness.

We see something we believe is wrong and we want to fix it. Maybe we see things in our husband we wish weren't there. Then we start nagging him. Do not become the woman in Proverbs who reminded her husband of a leaky roof:

> An endless dripping on a rainy day
> And a nagging wife are alike. Proverbs 27:15

Let us instead be the woman who lives by the principle in 1 Peter 3:1–2:

> In the same way, wives, submit yourselves to your own husbands so that, even if some disobey the Christian message, they may be won over without a message by the way their wives live when they observe your pure, reverent lives.

Remember the bad boy? You cannot change somebody who does not want to be transformed. More importantly, it's not your job to fix your husband, nor is it his job to fix you.

God created us. He knows every single thing about us—good and bad. Anything we think needs fixing, take it to Him because the best way to solve a problem is on our knees. Either it's going to get fixed in a way that does not have any repercussions, or we're going to be so focused on God we forget we had a problem. Either way, it's a win-win situation.

Journal

What are some of the things you think need fixing in your husband?

What are some of the things that need fixing in you? Take both lists to God in prayer. Look back at your lists (not obsessively, but at least once a year). I would love to hear the story of how God changed you (and your hubby) as you prayed.

Five

High School Sweethearts

The two really loved each other. They connected on such a level that they could figure out what the other was thinking with a look.

They had great plans to raise a large family because they both loved children. They looked forward to the day when they would have their first child and then the next and so forth.

As the years passed and no children came, they realized something was wrong. Had this happened today, the couple would have gone to the doctor and been tested to figure out where the problem lay.

There would have been fertility treatments and scheduled sexual relations.

There would have been mounting tension between the couple if treatments proved futile. There would have been blame as each accused the other for their childlessness.

But, it was clear the barrenness lay with Hannah. 1 Samuel 1:5 tells us the Lord had closed up her womb.

Elkanah had a second wife—Peninnah—who had sons and daughters. Oh, how that must have burned Hannah. She had to watch her rival raise children while she had none.

SHOW EMPATHY TO YOUR SPOUSE

↪ Read 1 Samuel 1:1–18

Challenges are a guarantee in marriage. We live in a sinful world and it takes much effort on the part of both persons to make a successful marriage.

The story of Elkanah and Hannah gives us a behind-the-scenes look at their family. Hannah was unable to bear children. In a society where children were considered a heritage, that was a big deal. It meant you had no one to inherit the plot of land that belonged to you. The land would pass instead to your closest relative. It meant your name would not be remembered. In a farming society, it meant servants or hired hands did chores instead of children.

"And you shall speak to the children of Israel, saying: 'If a man dies and has no son, then you shall cause his inheritance to pass to his daughter. If he has no daughter, then you shall give his inheritance to his brothers. If he has no brothers, then you shall give his inheritance to his father's brothers. And if his father has no brothers, then you shall give his inheritance to the relative closest to him in his family, and he shall possess it'" (Numbers 27:8–11).

As we read her story, we empathize with Hannah. She had to deal with the feeling of failure because she was unable to produce heirs for her husband. She had a jealous rival who provoked her. To make matters worse, her husband was completely oblivious.

"Hannah, why do you weep? Why do you not eat? And why is your heart grieved? Am I not better to you than ten sons?"

Elkanah may have thought he was being cute (by making a reference to the statement said to Naomi in Ruth 4:15). Instead, he appeared insensitive. He had to have known that Hannah wanted to be a mother more than anything else. He knew the inability to bear children degraded Hannah's worth in the eyes of her peers. Because he had children with Peninnah it was further proof (to Hannah at least), that it was all her fault.

When two people become one, what's important to one person should be significant to the other. As people who are cleaving together, we have to learn to sympathize when we can't empathize. Sympathy is a simple way to show the other person we care.

Journal

Make two lists of the things that are important to you and your husband. Are the things that are in your top five as critical to your spouse and vice versa?

Does your husband believe that you care about the things he cares about? Do you take time to listen to him (even when he starts a monologue about things you've heard a thousand times)? Do you expect him to listen to you when you do the same?

Don't be selfish; don't try to impress others. Be humble, thinking of others as better than yourselves (Philippians 2:3 NLT). If you put your husband first and he does the same, think about what an awesome marriage you would have.

BEWARE OF DISCONTENT

Alright, girlfriend, you love your husband and he loves you. Still, there are going to be times when you experience emotional pain in your marriage. Your husband may not be the source—though that can happen as well—the pain will come from many sources. You will have challenging days at work. The children will be difficult to handle and cause you to question your ability to parent. Your best friend may say something that hurts your feelings. As long as you're alive, numerous situations will test the limits of your patience and ability to cope.

We have to learn not to let these challenges compromise peace in our homes. Let's learn from Hannah. In the short scene, we walked with her through three trials:

- Provocation by Peninnah
- Insensitiveness from Elkanah
- An accusation by Priest Eli

Let's look at each one in detail.

Provocation by Peninnah

And her rival also provoked her severely, to make her miserable, because the Lord had closed her womb. So it was, year by year, when she went up to the house of the Lord, that she provoked her; therefore she wept and did not eat (1 Samuel 1:6–7).

The word translated as provoked is the Hebrew word ka`ac[1]. Kaas also translates as be angry, be grieved, take indignation, provoke to anger, unto wrath; to trouble; to grieve, rage, be indignant, be angry, be grieved, take indignation, provoke (to anger, unto wrath), have sorrow, vex, be wroth.

The word translated as miserable is the Hebrew word marah[2]. Marah could also mean: angry, bitterly chafed, discontented, great, or heavy.

The word provoked suggests there was some deliberate action. Peninnah went out of her way to make Hannah unhappy. She wanted to make Hannah discontent and angry with her life.

The Bible tells us Peninnah provoked Hannah because she was barren. Hannah's rival knew her weak spot. She knew what to say to make her sad. Doesn't that remind you of someone? The enemy knows each of us intimately. He tailors his attacks to suit our circumstances.

Picture it if you will:

The household had two adult females, one adult male and a lot of children. The walked into the house and the children swarmed him clamoring for attention. Sometimes he had a gift for them, and when he didn't, there was always a hug and a kind word.

One woman got a huge smacking kiss while the other stood on the fringes crowded out by the children. The recipient of the kiss cast a smug glance at the other woman as if to say, "See, I'm the one he loves because I'm have given him children." The other woman slipped quietly away, head bent and shoulders slumped. She would not let her rival see her tears today.

While we don't know the details of what happened in their home, the Bible tells us Hannah was miserable to the point of tears. She stopped eating and not even her favorite meals could tempt her. If you were Hannah what would you have done?

I'll tell you what I would have done: I would have made Peninnah at least half as miserable as she had made me. I would have grumbled and complained. My discontent would have spilled out of my mouth. My tongue would have become a weapon of mass destruction. Thankfully, I am not in the Bible. Instead, we have an example of temperance and grace under fire. Hannah kept her tongue and did not allow her unhappiness to spill out of her mouth.

Insensitiveness from Elkanah

Then Elkanah her husband said to her, "Hannah, why do you weep? Why do you not eat? And why is your heart grieved? Am I not better to you than ten sons?" (1 Samuel 1:8)

Elkanah noticed that Hannah was unhappy. He saw her tears and her inability to eat and tried to cheer her up. Unfortunately, the words he intended as a balm were as destructive as Peninnah's unkind words. A word of warning: this doesn't only happen in the Bible. Your husband will say things that have the opposite effect than he would have wanted. He may be trying to put a positive spin on a situation and say the wrong thing. Do not lash out at him when he does. If you do, please, apologize as soon as possible.

Men and women were created differently. Our values are not the same. No matter how in sync you are with your partner, you will have experiences he will not understand. A good man—one who walks with his Father—will listen and be supportive, but he may not get it. He won't understand why you need to cry. He won't comprehend your desire to chatter about what's bothering you until your vocabulary shrinks to words related only to "that thing". Please don't hold it against him. Don't blame him for whatever it is that you're going through (though you may believe he's responsible). Remember Adam and Eve? Blame gets us nowhere.

The accusation of Priest Eli

And it happened, as she continued praying before the Lord, that Eli watched her mouth. Now Hannah spoke in her heart; only her lips moved, but her voice was not heard. Therefore Eli thought she was drunk. So Eli said to her, "How long will you be drunk? Put your wine away from you!" (1 Samuel 1:12–14)

Poor girl. Her husband's side-wife was making her life miserable. Her insensitive husband had failed to realize the reason behind her unhappiness. As she poured out her heart to God, an unperceptive priest accused her of being drunk. Her, the same girl who couldn't bear to lift a fork of food to her mouth, much less drink enough alcohol to get drunk.

From Eli, we learn the lesson of not judging things, or people, based on how they appear. From Hannah, we learn to take every situation to God. Hannah knew that talking, nagging, and complaining (aka typical female responses), would have made it worse. Instead, she talked to God about it, as we should. He's never too busy. He will not get bored. He understands what you're going through, the reason for it and has the solution. He knows the lesson He's trying to teach and will take you to new places if only you would trust Him.

Journal

Make note of a situation in which your tongue made things worse. What could you have done? How can you prevent yourself from doing (or saying) the same thing again?

Note: a number of Bible verses on holding the tongue have been included at the end of this chapter.

A WOMAN OF HONOR KEEPS HER WORD

Hannah prayed for a son and in doing so made a vow to God. A vow which she kept. Can you imagine how hard it must have been for her to send away her only son? Hannah's sacrifice was a foreshadowing of God sending Jesus to die for humanity. Samuel served God's people in a capacity that should have been impossible for him. As an Ephraimite, he was exempt from serving in the temple. But God respected Hannah's sacrifice of her son. He honored her by giving Samuel the role of priest/prophet. Samuel was the first person to hold those dual roles.

You may be wondering what it means to be a woman of honor. Let us start by first answering the question, "What is honor?" Honor is a thing or person that brings respect, admiration or glory to another (person or thing). It is the quality of not only knowing, but doing what is morally right. So how does a woman of honor behave? I'm glad you asked. Before I can answer that question let me remind you that we are princesses chosen to represent a holy and majestic King. It means therefore that our behavior needs to be above reproach.

The Bible talks about honor and uses it to mean respect or reverence as in the following verses (the word honor is underlined):

"<u>Honor</u> your father and your mother, as the Lord your God has commanded you, that your days may be long, and that it may be well with you in the land which the Lord your God is giving you." Deuteronomy 5:16

"Then the Egyptians shall know that I am the Lord, when I have gained <u>honor</u> for Myself over Pharaoh, his chariots, and his horsemen." Exodus 14:18

"You shall do no injustice in judgment. You shall not be partial to the poor, nor <u>honor</u> the person of the mighty. In righteousness you shall judge your neighbor." Leviticus 19:15

Now Samuel took Saul and his servant and brought them into the hall, and had them sit in the place of <u>honor</u> among those who were invited; there were about thirty persons. 1 Samuel 9:22

We can infer from these verses that God desires honor for Himself and He expects us to treat others in an honorable way. A woman of honor knows what God expects from His people. She understands that she is His witness and must behave in a way that will draw positive attention to her Heavenly Father. People should want to be like her, they should seek out her company and over time, start to emulate her.

As God-girls, we become honorable women when we first learn to give respect to God. If we can obey Him, then we will be respectful to our parents, peers and those set in authority over us. We treat our husbands in the way God intended without resenting his authority. Like Hannah, we take our grouses to God and allow Him to reward us as He sees fit.

Journal

What does being an honorable woman mean to you? What actions or mindsets do you need to change to live up to that standard?

BIBLE VERSES ON HOLDING THE TONGUE

I don't know about you but sometimes I need a little help to hold my tongue. I have found these verses helpful because they remind me that my words have a greater effect than I may realize.

Let your speech always be with grace, seasoned with salt, that you may know how you ought to answer each one. Colossians 4:6

Let no corrupt word proceed out of your mouth, but what is good for necessary edification, that it may impart grace to the hearers. Ephesians 4:29

A wholesome tongue is a tree of life, but perverseness in it breaks the spirit Proverbs 15:4

Whoever guards his mouth and tongue keeps his soul from troubles. Proverbs 21:23

Set a guard, O Lord, over my mouth; keep watch over the door of my lips. Psalm 141:3

Even a fool is counted wise when he holds his peace; when he shuts his lips, he is considered perceptive. Proverbs 17:28

Death and life are in the power of the tongue, and those who love it will eat its fruit. Proverbs 18:21

For "He who would love life and see good days, let him refrain his tongue from evil, and his lips from speaking deceit." 1 Peter 3:10

If anyone among you thinks he is religious, and does not bridle his tongue but deceives his own heart, this one's religion is useless. James 1:26

Teach me, and I will hold my tongue; cause me to understand wherein I have erred. Job 6:24

The mouth of the righteous speaks wisdom, and his tongue talks of justice. Psalm 37:30

Not what goes into the mouth defiles a man; but what comes out of the mouth, this defiles a man. Matthew 15:11

So then, my beloved brethren, let every man be swift to hear, slow to speak, slow to wrath; for the wrath of man does not produce the righteousness of God. James 1:19–20

Six

When the Storms Come

Her children were dead. Seven sons, three daughters. Gone. Just like that. They hadn't been sick. If they had been sick, she would have been preparing and planning for their deaths. Instead, they died in a freakish accident.

All the money was gone. Every dollar they had saved. All their assets had been depleted. There was nothing left.

Now, her husband—the only person she had left to turn to—was covered in disgusting boils from head to feet. It was painful to look at him. What was the point of him being alive? He may as well be dead. At least then he'd be out of his misery and she wouldn't have to look at him.

Stay Connected to God

↛ Read Job 1:13–22 and Job 2:7–10

Unexpected things will happen. Because of sin we will suffer loss, despair, and hurt. What do we do when we face trials?

Wives and husband need to have an intimate relationship with their Heavenly Father.

Job and his wife were being attacked by the enemy. The Bible calls Job the servant of God (Job 1:8, 2:3), but not his wife. This suggests her relationship with Jehovah was not what it ought to have been.

The couple lost everything they valued—their wealth, their servants, and their children. The husband lost his health. Job, in his loss, first bows down in worship (Job 1:22), then starts complaining to God. Mrs. Job's response was:

"Do you still hold fast to your integrity? Curse God and die!" (Job 2:9)

Of the two, who do you think had a better relationship with God? As you read the book of Job, you will see a man who goes through a very vocal grieving process. He cursed the day he was born. He wished he had never grown to adulthood. He wished God would appear to him and give him a chance to defend himself. Through everything, he continued talking to God. Not once did he think to turn his back on Him.

My friend, your relationship with God is more critical than the one you have with your husband.

That's not what the world teaches. We're told our happiness is dependent on our husbands' ability to make us happy. We're taught that if they're not catering to our every need and desire, we should leave them and find someone who will. That's not what marriage looks like through God's eyes.

God didn't create a grown, capable man and an incapable, deficient woman. He created men to be caretakers and providers. Women were to help facilitate them in those roles. In the garden, God had a relationship with both the man and the woman. He expects the same thing today.

Journal

How's your relationship with your Heavenly Father? What can you do to improve it?

Have you ever been in a position where you failed to see God as your provider? Looking back at those events, can you see His provision?

MAINTAIN YOUR INTEGRITY

Integrity is the firm adherence to a code of moral or artistic values. It speaks about incorruptibility and remaining unimpaired by circumstances.

The original Hebrew word for integrity is tummah[1] which could have been translated as innocence. The word tummah appears only five times in the Old Testament and four of them occur in Job[1]. As you read through the verses below, replace the word integrity with innocence (the word integrity is underlined):

Then the LORD said to Satan, "Have you considered My servant Job, that there is none like him on the earth, a blameless and upright man, one who fears God and shuns evil? And still, he holds fast to his <u>integrity</u>, although you incited Me against him, to destroy him without cause." Job 2:3

Then his wife said to him, "Do you still hold fast to your <u>integrity</u>? Curse God and die!" Job 2:9

Far be it from me
that I should say you are right;
Till I die I will not put away my <u>integrity</u> from me.
Job 27:5

Let me be weighed on honest scales,
that God may know my <u>integrity</u>. Job 31:6

The <u>integrity</u> of the upright will guide them,
But the perversity of the unfaithful will destroy them.
Proverbs 11:3

Throughout his experiences, Job maintained his innocence. Job's friends offended him by interpreting the unfortunate events in his life as punishment for his sins. They felt he deserved it. Yet, in his trials, his standards did not change.

Journal

What are your core values? When the storms of life come, how well do you adhere to them? Do you hold fast to your values as Job did? Or do you open your hands and allow them to scatter in the wind at the first sign of trouble?

God respects integrity. It was one of the things He commended Job for. It was one of the reasons Satan hated him. Integrity is one of the precepts that will guide us into acting according to God's commands.

YOUR VALUE IS INTRINSIC

I grew up thinking that something outside of myself would make me happy. The right grades, perfect outfit, a good job, a husband, a family, the whatever— would make me "good enough". Did you have a similar experience? Did you grow up thinking you needed something external to make you valuable?

In a society where everything is a click away, it's easy to buy into the lie that our value comes from material things. Women are taught that her Prince Charming is waiting in an unexpected place—the library, supermarket, church—she only needs to find him. These teachings make it easy to believe we need a man to make us happy or to complete us.

There are some who believe a woman is not valuable unless she's in a relationship. Okay, let me dispel the myth: you are not somebody's other half.

You are a whole person created in the image of a whole God. You do not need someone to complete you. Your husband does not need someone to complete him. Both of you are complete in Jesus (Colossians 2:10).

Alright, let that sink in for a minute.

When something is complete it doesn't lack anything. It has everything that it needs. Did you get that? When you were created, you lacked nothing. You were complete—are complete—in Christ. Your value is intrinsic because it comes from God. In God's eyes you are:

- Chosen, royal, holy—1 Peter 2:9
- Bought with a price—1 Corinthians 6:20
- His child—1 John 3:1
- Accepted—Romans 15:7
- Conqueror—Romans 8:37
- Precious—every hair on your head is numbered Matthew 10:30
- The apple of God's eye—Zechariah 2:8

Journal

What are some of the other things the Bible says about you? Make a list using the personal pronoun: "I am".

Seven

Stolen Moments

Her monthly period had ended. As was customary, she had gone through the purification process. Then she had a bath. Her husband, who was in the king's army, was away fighting.

When she came out of her bath, there were messengers from the king. She had been summoned. What could he want with her?

She soon found out. She went to the palace, where the king slept with her. Sometime after she *returned home, she realized she was pregnant. She sent a message to the king.*

BE FAITHFUL TO YOUR SPOUSE

↳ Read 2 Samuel 11:1-5

We read Bathsheba's story and judge her for sleeping with David. As a wife, you may think there's no way you could cheat on your husband and that's a great place to stand. But I'm sure you've heard cheating is one of the main reasons for divorce[1].

Such an innocent-sounding word, isn't it? Cheat. We say someone cheats when they have some form of intimate contact with a person other than their significant other. In a more traditional sense, cheating means to defraud or deceive someone.

When we are unfaithful to our spouses, we break the vow of commitment we made to them. We defraud them by giving to someone else what is theirs. And in the majority of cases, there's also lying involved. Bathsheba and David committed adultery. To cover it up, David tried to get Uriah to sleep with Bathsheba. David was hoping when Bathsheba had the baby, Uriah would think it was his.

When the plan failed, David gave Uriah a death sentence. This faithful foot soldier brought his own sentence to the executioner. What did Joab think when he read David's letter? I bet whatever he thought the answer became clear when David married Bathsheba. David tried to deceive Uriah and violated his responsibility as Uriah's king. This violation of trust becomes more evident when we examine their history.

USE WISDOM

Did you notice that David's inquiry about Bathsheba resulted in a mini-genealogy? She was "Bathsheba, the daughter of Eliam, the wife of Uriah the Hittite" (2 Samuel 11:3). Why do you think that was the answer he received?

↠ Read 2 Samuel 23:8–39

This passage chronicles the great warriors who had left Israel during Saul's reign to join David in exile. There was a group of warriors known as "The Thirty" (2 Samuel 3:13). Bathsheba's father Eliam and her husband Uriah were a part of this group (2 Samuel 23: 24, 34 & 39). That Bathsheba was Mrs. Uriah was enough reason for David not to have pursued her. But when he heard those two names connected with the woman he was lusting after, he had extra reasons to be cautious. Uriah and Eliam deserved his respect. They supported him when many people did not. David's disregard for these two warriors shows the impact of sin. Sin destroys. It demolishes relationships and friendships. It destroys lives.

In his lust, David could not see the impact his actions would have on those around him. We need to learn from David that we should act with wisdom.

God gives us the ability to discern right from wrong. Proverbs 2:6 tells us the Lord gives wisdom; from His mouth come knowledge and understanding. When we connect with God, we see His warnings when we are going in the wrong direction. When we get disconnected from God, sin obliterates our better judgment.

Journal

Write of an experience when you had wanted something outside of God's will. What were the signs? How have you grown from the experience? What can you do in the future to protect yourself from acting foolishly?

OCCUPY YOUR TIME WISELY

Growing up, my mother taught me the "devil made work for idle hands". I learned when I don't occupy myself in legitimate activities, I get into trouble.

The passage starts, "in the spring of the year, when kings normally go out to war, David sent Joab and the Israelite army to fight the Ammonites" (2 Samuel 11:1 NLT).

If you read the previous chapter, you learn this wasn't an insignificant skirmish. The Israelites were defending the dignity and honor of their people. They had a limited time to fight as there were only a few, short months before the rainy season began.

Jerusalem did not have asphalted roads. Rain meant muddy roads and impossible travel conditions for chariots, horses, and soldiers. Besides, these men needed to be home to help with the plowing. This was no time for the king to be slacking off. David should have been on the battlefield leading his men to victory. He shouldn't have been on his roof peeping at his neighbor's wife. And when he saw her, he should have walked away. He should not have slept with Uriah's wife. When we don't occupy ourselves with wholesome activities, we do things we should not do.

Protect Your Modesty

Much of Bathsheba's history is not included in the biblical account. We don't know whether she was being modest while she bathed. We don't know if she willingly slept with David or if he coerced her.

She could have felt she had no choice because he was king. Or, she may have been flattered because he was king. Did she feel ashamed after the fact? Did she wonder what her husband would think or how he would feel if he knew? Nobody knows. All her emotions and thoughts are lost to us. All we have left is this statement:

"Then David sent messengers to get her; and when she came to the palace, he slept with her. She had just completed the purification rites after having her menstrual period. Then she returned home" (2 Samuel 11:4 NLT).

Bathsheba's story gives us a powerful reason to act appropriately at all times. We have to choose to be modest. In other words: we have to act married. When we're married, courting, or in a committed relationship, our behavior should reflect that. It's inappropriate to flirt and be seductive or coy with persons who are not our partners. Such behavior is not okay at any time for us God-girls. It's especially distasteful when we are in a committed relationship.

People should be able to tell at least two things by our interaction with others:

1. We belong to God
2. We are committed to another person

Modesty speaks to the way we act, the way we speak. It includes the things we talk about and how we dress.

In a society where people dress "as bare as they dare" and say whatever comes to mind, it's hard to stand on principles. However, if we are to be good ambassadors of our Heavenly Father, the King of kings, being modest is a small thing to do. Modesty begins in the mind. We have to think clean, pure thoughts if we are to act and live prudently. Thinking clean becomes easier the longer we spend interacting with God's word. As we spend time alone with Him, we learn to meditate on things that are pure.

If we run our behavior and our dress code through the filter of Philippians 4:8 it might look something like this:

- Is this (dress/behavior) a true representation of my identity in Christ?
- Am I acting as if I were a princess?
- Does my behavior or dress reflect purity?
- Is my attitude praiseworthy?
- If I saw this dress on someone with my body type, would it be flattering?
- Would a virtuous woman wear this?
- If it meets all these criteria, awesome. If it doesn't, ask yourself what needs to change. Take the steps to modify the behavior or clothing.

Journal

What does "acting married" mean to you? Write down the tips you would give if someone asked.

How would you encourage a young lady to protect her modesty?

YOUR SHAME DOES NOT HAVE TO CRIPPLE YOU

Do you know the woman in Proverbs 31? Of course, you do. If you don't, there's a chapter in this book talking about her but don't skip ahead.

Proverbs 31:10–31 remain as that sometimes elusive standard of a godly wife. Sometimes we feel as though we can never measure up to her. We will never be perfect enough to be considered a virtuous woman.

You may be wondering what the Proverbs 31 woman and Bathsheba have in common. That's a great question, I'm glad you asked. Would you believe Bathsheba wrote the description of the woman in Proverbs 31? Let's examine the evidence.

Proverbs 31:1 reads:

"The words of King Lemuel, the utterance which his mother taught him." Proverbs 1:1 tells us the book represents "the proverbs of Solomon the son of David, king of Israel."

While there is some debate over the identity of King Lemuel, commentators Benson, Jamieson, Fausset and Brown believe that Lemuel could refer to Solomon as the name means of or from God, or belonging to God. Lemuel has a similar meaning to Jedidiah which is the name God gave to Solomon because He loved him[2] (2 Samuel 12:24–25).

So, how did Bathsheba go from being an adulteress to the woman who wrote "who can find a virtuous woman?"

↪ Read 2 Samuel 11:5, 14–27

Bathsheba was pregnant by a man who was not her spouse. According to Mosaic Law, she should have been killed. The penalty for adultery was death by stoning, for both of them. Did she know her husband had returned home shortly after she had told the king she was pregnant? The Bible doesn't say. Was she aware of the elaborate measures taken by David to cover up their sin? It seems unlikely. But we know when Bathsheba heard Uriah her husband was dead, she mourned for him (2 Samuel 11:26). She lived through the loss of her spouse—a good man who died as a cover up for her sin.

She birthed a child born a scant nine months after her husband had gone to war. There would have been those who believed Uriah had impregnated her before he left. There would have been some who knew she had a period after her husband had left. They would have known she had spent hours alone in a room with David. They would have known Uriah came home briefly and had not spent any time at home with her.

People would have wondered why David married her after her husband's death. Did he do it out of pity because her husband died under his watch? Why then didn't he marry all the widows of his soldiers who died in battle? Her baby would have been the source of gossip and contention as he grew older. Did she try to wish away his existence?

And then he died. Seven days after his birth. As she buried him, maybe she understood his death was because of her sin. Bathsheba's mistakes did not end there.

↳ Read 1 Kings 2:13–25.

Adonijah wanted to marry David's concubine, Abishag. He asked Bathsheba to secure Solomon's permission on his behalf. Solomon's response was, "Why are you asking for Abishag to be wed to Adonijah? You may as well ask for him to be given the kingdom as well" (1 Kings 2:22).

To understand the meaning of this scene, it's important to know the context. In 1 Kings 1, David had promised Solomon would succeed him as king. This was God's desire. Solomon was not the eldest son and so the title did not automatically fall to him.

Adonijah, as Solomon's older brother, would have been closer to the crown. He had attempted to usurp the throne while King David lay on his deathbed. Had it not been for the quick action of Nathan the prophet, Adonijah would have been king. David affirmed Solomon's right to the throne and Solomon succeeded his father.

As was customary at the time, Solomon would have inherited his father's harem. He would not take them as his wives because that would have meant uncovering his father's nakedness. At the same time, because he was king, he was responsible for their welfare. If Adonijah married Abishag, it would have been tantamount to saying he had a legal right to the throne. The result would have been a civil war.

Adonijah would then have the opportunity to openly oppose Solomon. Bathsheba was completely clueless. Can you imagine the things she said to herself? Stupid. Can't do anything right.

Thankfully, Solomon saw through the scheme. Adonijah received the death sentence because of his request. Here was yet another person who lost his life because of Bathsheba; at least, that's how she could have seen it. It would have been easy for Bathsheba to become bitter and disillusioned. She could have turned her back on God because of shame. Instead, she chose to go on. She learned from her experiences.

She wrote the words in Proverbs 31 so her son could learn from her. Today, we have her words to encourage us.

Do you think Bathsheba saw herself as a virtuous woman? I believe she did, and that she wanted her son to know the negative things in a woman's past do not define her. A woman can choose to walk away from the ashes of her past and build a new life. My friend, the things you did in the past do not have to define you.

God allowed the words of Proverbs 31 to be in the Bible to encourage His daughters to see ourselves as He does. We may have been dishonest, immodest, and indecent but we don't have to stay that way. We can choose to believe our past does not define our present selves and doesn't represent who we will be in the future.

Journal

Are there things in your past that make you feel ashamed? Put them before God and ask for forgiveness if you hadn't done so before. Ask Him to heal you from past wounds and the freedom to walk boldly into the future He has prepared for you.

How has your past impacted the person you are today? Celebrate the lessons learned and the woman you are today.

Pause to Reflect

Is There Grace in Your Marriage?

Grace, in a nutshell, is the undeserved kindness God displays towards mankind. We do nothing to earn it, it is freely given. As Christians, we love to claim God's grace, especially when we know we've done something wrong. But—

Do we practice grace with the person closest to us—our spouse? Do we show grace to our husbands? Do they show grace to us? Are the things they did to hurt us wiped away with love? Are we quick to forgive? Do we forgive with grace? Or do we hang on to past hurt like spiders clinging to webs?

Do the "sins" of our spouses show up as unwelcome visitors in our marriages?

Grace towards our partner should be evident in our willingness to work for the marriage we want. Yes, things may not be going as we expected (especially in the early years), but do we resolve to keep trying?

Do we purpose not to keep score of offenses made? Do we practice the type of forgiveness expressed in Matthew 18:21–22 and forgive 70 times seven every single day?

Prayer

Lord, I long for grace in my marriage, the kind of grace You display to us. Help me to speak health, life, and truth into my marriage. In Jesus' name, Amen.

Journal

Write down some ways in which you can show grace to your hubby.

Eight

This Is Not a Hollywood Marriage

He was their miracle child—the son they never thought they would have. For years they had wanted children, but she was barren. Long after she had given up on having babies, an angel told her she would have a son.

This child had a huge responsibility. He would begin to deliver his people from their oppressive rulers. She was ecstatic though it meant she could not have certain foods. Her child was to be a Nazirite—a person consecrated to the Lord. He was to adhere to the Nazirite diet. His beautiful hair grew thick and long. They never trimmed a single strand from his *head. The time came when he was old enough to marry. But instead of choosing one of the beautiful Israelite girls, he wanted to marry a Philistine woman.*

A VOW HAS MEANING

✤ Read Judges 14:1–9

We use the words "I promise" and "I swear" to show people we are being serious. Half the time, we forget about the thing we promised seconds after we've said the words. This was not the case in the society where Samson grew up.

Nazirite is the translation of the Hebrew word naziyr[1] meaning separate or consecrated to. It comes from the root word nazaar which means to hold aloof, abstain from food and drink, from impurity even from divine worship, to set apart, devote or separate. A Nazirite was someone consecrated to God.

In Numbers 6:1–21, God gives specific instructions concerning the Nazirite. In short, a Nazirite should:

- Abstain from wine and similar drink.
- Avoid vinegar made from wine or any similar drink, grape juice, grapes or anything produced by the vine.
- Allow his hair to grow for the duration of his vow.

- Not make himself unclean. This includes staying away from dead bodies including members of his family.

The law of the vow which is found in Numbers 30 can be summed up thus:

"When you make a vow to the Lord your God, you shall not delay to pay it; for the Lord your God will surely require it of you, and it would be sin to you. But if you abstain from vowing, it shall not be sin to you. That which has gone from your lips you shall keep and perform, for you voluntarily vowed to the Lord your God what you have promised with your mouth" (Deuteronomy 23:21–23).

A Nazirite made a vow to God, one he had to keep. In Samson's case, the declaration came from God. He was, however, under the same obligation to keep the promise as if he had made it himself.

"This is the law of the Nazirite who vows to the Lord the offering for his separation, and besides that, whatever else his hand is able to provide; according to the vow which he takes, so he must do according to the law of his separation" (Numbers 6:21).

Samson made the decision to get married. God had forbidden the Israelites to intermarry with the nations around them. As such, Samson should have chosen an Israelite woman. Instead, he chose a Philistine. As a Nazirite and an Israelite, this woman would have been off-limits.

Samson's behavior makes you wonder if he knew the rules surrounding the lifestyle of a Nazirite. He should have known the importance of keeping himself pure. But we see him choosing to marry a heathen. We also see him touching the dead body of an unclean animal and eating food which came in contact with it.

At first, I thought ignorance was the reason for Solomon's actions until I realized he chose not to tell his parents. His choice was deliberate. Because he had broken his Nazirite vow, he would have had to shave his head. He would have lost his supernatural strength and become an ordinary man.

As God-girls, we've made vows too. We pledged to serve God and to treat our husbands with the respect God expects. We promised to live up to the example of our Savior Jesus. Sometimes as a wife, these promises are hard to keep. And yes, sometimes we do break them. Thankfully, when we do it's not necessary for us to shave our heads, but we do need to repent and make an effort to be more faithful in the future.

Samson and his wife remind us that we need to understand the intent behind the promises we make. We should learn not to make vows without thinking. Our husbands should be able to able to believe us when we give our word. Even if *they* don't, God should know us as faithful women.

Journal

Do you make promises lightly? How good are you at keeping your word? Make a list of the promises you have made but not kept (at least those you can remember).

Make a decision to either fulfill those promises or seek absolution. Speak with the person to whom you made the promise and explain why you did not keep your word. If both parties agree, take the necessary steps to fulfill the promise.

KEEP YOUR VOWS TO GOD

Marriage is one of the greatest pledges you can make in the presence of God. By doing so, we tell Him we agree with His vision for a married couple. We agree to leave and cleave. We commit to treating our spouses in the manner God proposes.

Hollywood wants us to believe the Vegas marriage and the quickie divorce are normal. They are not God's intent. God was explicit, He hates divorce (Malachi 2:16). Jesus, while on earth, told the Pharisees:

"Moses, because of the hardness of your hearts, permitted you to divorce your wives, but from the beginning, it was not so" (Matthew 19:8).

Allow me to clarify: this is not an instruction to stay with an abusive spouse. If you are in that situation, please seek professional help. Do not lament and say: "Oh, God hates divorce, so I am stuck in this relationship." God hates the practice of divorce. He does not hate the divorcée. God may dislike a particular practice, but He understands why some things happen. If all spouses treated their partners as God intended, divorce would not exist.

While many couples choose to write unique vows, the essence of each marriage vow remains the same:

"I, ___, take thee, ___, to be my wedded husband/wife, to have and to hold, from this day forward, for better, for worse, for richer, for poorer, in sickness and in health, to love and to cherish, till death do us part, according to God's holy ordinance; and thereto I pledge thee my faith [or] pledge myself to you[2]."

Saying these words on your wedding day felt romantic and idealistic, but a lot of effort is needed to keep them. Let's break it down together:

I, (insert your name), take, (insert your husband's name), to be my wedded husband

The word take suggests a choice. You made a conscious decision to marry the man you did. Circumstances may have dictated it, but you had a choice.

The decision to wed is a choice to unite in marriage. It speaks about permanence and commitment. The man and his wife join forces. Their union is exclusive of everyone, including parents and children.

to have and to hold

Let's look at some more definitions:

We say we have something when we take possession of it. It may refer to an experience, a thought or a physical thing.

To hold is to grasp or capture something (or someone). It also suggests support.

Don't you find it's interesting that take, have and hold can be used interchangeably? These are simple words which we use every day. Yet their meanings, when applied to marriage give them new significance.

When we decide to get married, we agree to support, to hold fast, to accept, to receive and to experience our partner.

from this day forward for better, for worse, for richer, for poorer, in sickness and in health

There is permanence here. The vow is not for the next two months or until he makes me mad. It's a commitment to a person on their best days and on their worst. They make the same commitment to us. As women, we are taught we should be cared for by our spouses—and we love that part—but it's not always easy to reciprocate.

Nonetheless, we agreed to it. Surrounded by our beautiful, wedding finery, we said yes to a lifetime of loyalty to this man.

to love and to cherish

As we have already seen, the greatest definition of love is found in the Bible: "Greater love has no one than this than to lay down one's life for his friends" (John 15:13). Are you willing to die for your spouse?

Let me take you off the spot by answering the question first: I don't know if I am. It seems like a disloyal answer—I love my husband, but if I chose to die for him does it mean I love him more than I love God? Would dying for my spouse be an acceptable sacrifice in God's eyes? I don't know the answers and because I don't, I am glad God doesn't ask us to die to prove our faithfulness to our spouses.

Instead, He lays out a guideline in 1 Corinthians 13:4–8 about what love should look like. He told wives to be submissive and husbands to love in Ephesians 5:22–33. Through God's eyes, a strong marriage is one where both partners respect and love each other.

We pledged to cherish our partner. To cherish someone is to appreciate them. We can't treasure what we don't love. What we cherish we will care for; we will keep it close and nurture it.

Are you cherishing your spouse? What have you done to show your love in the past 24 hours? (It still counts if this question was your prompt to do something nice.)

till death do us part

This part is self-explanatory. Marriage should be permanent. We don't get a ticket out for minor or major inconveniences. There's no return policy, we can't bring it back because it doesn't fit or it's out of style.

according to God's holy ordinance

And there it is. All the things we agreed to do: the having, holding and the taking, we do so according to God's holy ordinance.

Holy: specially recognized as or declared sacred by religious use or authority; consecrated

Ordinance: an authoritative rule or law; a decree or command.

and thereto I pledge thee my faith [or] pledge myself to you

When we said those words to our husbands we promised our faithfulness. This includes our commitment to the relationship and our fidelity

That's a lot, isn't it? Who knew less than 60 words could have so much meaning and involve such a depth of commitment?

Journal

Think about the vows you made to your spouse, where have you fallen short? What areas do you need to improve on?

DON'T BE A NAG

Okay, girl, let's talk about nagging. I get it, I really do. Your husband doesn't listen and so you have to remind him of the things he doesn't want to do over and over again. So yes, let me add my voice to the choir: nagging doesn't work. Believe me, I've tried. All that happens is your husband learns to tune you out and you start to annoy yourself. Remember the "dripping" woman in Proverbs 27:15? Let's not aspire to be her.

↷ Read Judges 14:10–20

The couple had made their vows and was at the reception with their guests. During the week-long feast, Samson posed a riddle to his guests:
"Out of the eater comes something to eat.
Out of the strong comes something sweet" (Judges 14:14).
Samson knew no one could have guessed the answer. I imagine him feeling superior thinking he was smarter than everyone else. He had a smug, little smirk on his face as he listened to the answers. One by one, each guest attempted to solve the riddle.

I imagine Mrs. Samson admiring her husband's big muscles and thinking about how jealous her friends must be. He was so clever. It was impossible to guess the answer to his riddle; even her most intelligent friends were silent.

After three days, some men approached Mrs. Samson and threatened to kill her and her father. They gave her a choice: her life and her father's in exchange for her help. To learn the answer to the riddle and protect her father, Mrs. Samson became very vocal (and whiny).

"You don't love me." Drip. "You hate me." Drip. "How could you ask a riddle and not tell me the answer?" Drip. Drip. Drip. And on and on she went. For four days.

Have you ever had a child badger you for something? Can you imagine how much more annoying it is when an adult does it? On the seventh day, Samson told her the answer because "she tormented him with her nagging" (Judges 14:16).

Samson's Hollywood marriage lasted seven days before crumbling under the weight of a whine. Girlfriend, nagging can be detrimental to your marriage. Do not give in to the urge to whine and nag. Bite your tongue (gently) if you have to. Better a sore tongue than an unhappy spouse.

Journal

Do you whine and complain a lot? If your answer is yes, why? What's your plan to reduce your whining?

WHO ARE YOU LOYAL TO?

Everything was fine until some of the guests threatened to kill Mrs. Samson and her father. Then she had a dilemma: should she remain loyal to her husband? Or should she save herself and her father? The relationship between Mr. and Mrs. Samson was based on the superficial. The first challenge they experienced destroyed their marriage. The lesson for us is that we need to base our marriages on something more substantial than sexual attraction. If lust was the foundation for your union, you need to work on creating a more stable base.

A good start is trying to figure out where your loyalties lie. Your first commitment should be to Jehovah. Your next obligation should be to your spouse. Neither Samson nor his wife had any idea what it meant to be in a committed relationship. Mrs. Samson betrayed her husband's secret to protect her father. Later, we see Samson forsaking his wife and returning to his parents. In both cases, it was a matter of intimacy.

Samson had chosen her because he liked the way she looked and he desired her. We don't know her reasons, but it is clear neither of them made an effort to leave and cleave.

My friend, it's tempting to lean on your family especially if they are supportive. But, after your marriage, your loyalty is to your husband and later your children. Through God's eyes, a man leaves his parents and cleaves to his wife. The expectation for wives is the same: it requires a shift of loyalty.

A good way of showing allegiance to your spouse is to keep private things private and secret things secret. Let us not be untrustworthy wives, because you know what, an untrustworthy spouse is worse than a leaky faucet.

Journal

Are you a trustworthy spouse? If you have faltered in this area, how can you improve?

Nine

Miracles Happen

They had spent their entire adult life together. Life had been good. He served as a priest in the temple of the Most High God.

They only had one complaint: they had no children. For years they had prayed but it hadn't happened and now it was too late. They were both much too old to become parents.

One day, while he was burning incense before the Lord in the temple, an angel appeared to him. "Do not be afraid," the angel said to him, "for your prayer has been heard; and your wife will bear you a son."

Imagine his surprise. He had an encounter with an angel and he was going to have a son? The thing he and his wife had prayed for was going to happen? It was unbelievable—such a thing was no longer possible, was it?

WHEN YOU PRAY FOR A MIRACLE – BELIEVE

✢ Read Luke 1:5–25

There's one thing people always say about prayer: it can work miracles. As Christians, it is assumed that we are all great prayer warriors because we pray always and without ceasing. The truth is, a lot of times prayer is our last resort instead of our first option. Why?

As we look at the story of Zacharias and his wife Elizabeth, we see a couple who prayed for something to happen. It never did. At least, it didn't happen in the timeframe they had expected. Did they stop praying? I think they prayed as long as it was possible for Elizabeth to become pregnant, then they stopped. They learned to accept that they would not have the child they desired.

You will have a lot of wants in your life. There will be things you desire for yourself, your spouse, and your marriage. I pray you will bring your request to God first and not after you have exhausted all the alternatives. Believe me when I tell you it's a lot easier to write those words than it is to practice them, but I know prayer works.

The key thing about prayer is this: whatever you are asking God for, you have to believe He can give it to you. We believe God is superior to us. At the same time, it is important to understand we will never know how His mind works.

We try to explain God's motivations and actions by comparing Him to ourselves. What we should do instead is seek to understand the principles by which God operates. One such principle is: if you ask for something, believe it can happen.

We read in James 1:5:

If any of you lacks wisdom, let him ask of God, who gives to all liberally and without reproach, and it will be given to him. But let him ask in faith, with no doubting, for he who doubts is like a wave of the sea driven and tossed by the wind. For let not that man suppose that he will receive anything from the Lord; he is a double-minded man, unstable in all his ways.

In this scenario, a person asks for wisdom. The principle is: without faith, he will not receive his desire though God is able to provide it.

Let's look at a few more verses:

"Ask, and it will be given to you; seek, and you will find; knock, and it will be opened to you" (Matthew 7:7).

The principle here is persistence. If we want something, we have to ask for it many times. Yes, God knows what we want before we ask, but it doesn't mean He will always grant it to us *before* we ask.

"And whatever things you ask in prayer, believing, you will receive" (Matthew 21:22).

Again, the principle here is faith. How can we expect to receive anything if we don't believe it's possible? Long after you think it is probable, continue to believe it is possible with God. I don't want you to think everything you pray fervently for you will receive as long as you pray in faith. That's not how it works. Let's go back to James:

You do not have because you do not ask. You ask and do not receive, because you ask amiss, that you may spend it on your pleasures (James 4:2a–3).

Not every prayer will be answered in the affirmative. God can grant us the desires of our hearts, but it has to line up with His plans for us. He's not going to give us something today if it will jeopardize our salvation in the future. As a God-girl, you have to know how to pray in earnest and with faith while accepting that God's will supersedes yours. God is fair, He treats all His children the same and we are all His children.

We read about Sarah and Elizabeth two women who had babies long after the time for child-bearing had passed. Yet, God was able to bless both of them by giving them the baby they desired. Hannah, Rachel, Rebekah, the Shunamite woman, and Manoah's wife also had babies though they were barren. The lesson here for us is that God does not discriminate.

Many times, as women we tend to underestimate how much God loves us. The enemy would have us believe God can answer the prayers of everyone, but not ours.

My friend, that is not true. When the enemy tells you that lie, remind him God does not show favoritism (Romans 2:11). God loves each of us with the same passion and fervor.

At times, your husband will get discouraged. He may begin to wonder if God is not answering his prayers because he does not deserve it. I want you to remind him, dear friend, that our Heavenly Father answers all prayers in His own time and His own way. God gives us His favor. We don't earn it.

As a woman walking with God, you will learn you can't do anything in your own strength. You have to pray your way through. As a wife, your prayer list goes up exponentially. You pray for wisdom, patience, and grace. You pray as you learn things about yourself that you never knew before. Marriage stretches boundaries you never knew you had.

Praying for your husband is going to be a critical part of your married life. Early in my marriage, I was having a conversation with my husband. The details elude me, but I remember feeling annoyed because he was being stubborn. I felt mean words bubbling up out of my mouth (oh don't look at me like that; it will happen to you, too). I buttoned my lips and said "Lord, this man is testing my patience help him to realize—"

A few seconds after I opened my eyes, my husband turned and looked at me. "Were you praying for me?" he asked.

"I was," I replied. "Why do you ask?"

"Because God told me I was the reason you were praying."

My dear friend, it doesn't always happen this way. I used this example because I wanted you to see that our God cares about every nuance of our lives. He is willing and able to come to our rescue if we invite Him into our lives. We have to ask Him to be a part of our journey.

Journal

What do you want God to do in your marriage today? Write a prayer with your request. As you do, believe God is capable of blessing you beyond your imagination.

Pause to Reflect

The Ten Commandments of Marriage

1. God, Father, Son, and Holy Spirit, should be at the center of your marriage. If God is not at the center of our lives, our relationships (including our marriages) will fail.

2. There should be no idols in your marriage. Not success, money, work, children, power, or any other idol should be placed above your marriage.

3. You and your family should take time each week to rest and worship together. Praise God for your marriage.

4. Honor your parents and your parents-in-law. Honor your husband in his role as a father. The wife should be honored in her role as a mother.

5. Death and life are in the power of the tongue; do not use your tongue to tear down your spouse.

6. Do not have an emotional, physical or sexual relationship with someone who is not your spouse.

7. Do not deplete your partner's emotional bank account. Your deposits should be greater than your withdrawals.

8. Do not over-state expenses to get "extra" money. Do not "borrow" money from his wallet. Do not take money from your wife's purse without her permission or knowledge.

9. Do not tell lies about your spouse. Do not exaggerate their flaws or their abilities.

10. Do not lust after someone who is not your spouse. Do not wish for someone else's bank account, figure, looks, job or for anything that is not yours.

Prayer

Lord, thank You for the reminder that You are to be at the heart of everything I do. I invite the presence of the Holy Spirit into my life and my marriage. In Jesus' name. Amen.

Journal

Which one of God's law is most difficult for you to blend into your marriage?

Ten

Looks Can Be Deceiving

She was engaged. Although the wedding wouldn't happen for a few months, her family was busy getting things ready. They loved celebrating and a wedding was a great excuse for a party.

When the angel appeared to her she was shocked. She was to be the Messiah's mother? How could that happen? She was still a virgin. Her first child would be a boy. Her people would consider her blessed.

How would her future husband react when he found out she was already pregnant?

Following God Won't Always Be Easy

↳ Read Luke 1:26–45

We modern gals love the story of the virgin birth. We see it as a sign of the power of Almighty God and it is. Mary was excited to be the Messiah's mother. She grew up knowing the prophecy that the Savior of her people would be born from a virgin:

Therefore, the Lord Himself will give you a sign: Behold, the virgin shall conceive and bear a Son, and shall call His name Immanuel (Isaiah 7:14).

To be the virgin mother of the Messiah was a great honor. When the angel gave her the news, she was amenable. We know she was receptive to the Lord's leading because of her response in Luke 1:38:

"Let it be to me according to your word."

What we modern girls may not have considered is this significant truth: Mary wasn't married to Joseph yet. They were betrothed. In modern language, we would say they were engaged. A pregnancy before the marriage would have been a good reason for him not to marry her. In fact, we read in Matthew 1:19–20 that Joseph was considering a divorce.

Then Joseph her husband, being a just man, and not wanting to make her a public example, was minded putting her away secretly (Matthew 1:19).

Today, it's a norm for single women to be mothers. But for Mary, things would have been different. In a society where women did not work to earn a living, she would have had to depend on the kindness of others. She would have had to go out and glean the fields to get food for herself and her child, had she been allowed to live.

As an unmarried mother, she would have been ostracized. In Genesis 38:24, when Tamar became pregnant, Judah wanted to have her burned to death. Mary would have known this story. She may have wondered what punishment she would have received.

Despite all this, Mary was willing, even eager, to be the mother of the Messiah. Let's read the first few lines of her song which we find in Luke 1:46–55:

"My soul magnifies the Lord,
And my spirit has rejoiced in God my Savior.
For He has regarded the lowly state of His maidservant;
For behold, henceforth all generations will call me blessed.
For He who is mighty has done great things for me.
And holy is His name" (Luke 1:46–49).

Mary was not thinking about the challenges ahead. No, she focused on the future blessing. Are you a Mary? Do you find joy in future blessings? Or do you focus on the present difficulties?

"Count it all joy," James says, "when you go through various trials" (James 1:2). He was not telling us to laugh hysterically when we are going through a tough time; he was telling us we needed to learn to look beyond the present trouble. We should instead think about how we can grow from the test, instead of wondering when it will end.

As a wife, you are going to have to deal with challenging things. Your faith will be tested. Your patience will be stretched beyond the point of endurance. You and your spouse will go through difficult periods in your marriage. You may find yourself wondering why you got married in the first place.

As long as you are walking in obedience to God and doing what He has asked you to do, hold on. It's not always easy to follow God, but with the help of the Holy Spirit, it is possible.

Journal

What is God asking you to do today? Is this something you think will be easy for you? Why or why not? Document the challenges you believe you will face as you try to be obedient.

Write a prayer asking God to help you with those things.

A GOOD MAN FOLLOWS GOD

↪ Read Matthew 1:18–25 and Luke 1:39–45, 56

As soon as she received the news from the Holy Spirit, Mary went to visit her cousin Elizabeth. We know she was already pregnant because when Elizabeth saw Mary, the baby in her womb "leaped with joy" (Luke 1:44). Elizabeth prophesied and expressed her great joy to see the mother of her Messiah.

Mary remained with Elizabeth for three months. During this time, she may have started experiencing early pregnancy symptoms such as tiredness and bloating. She may have been urinating more than usual. Did she experience mood swings, nausea, and tender or swollen breasts?

Mary would have become more aware of the baby growing inside her body. This may have been a time for her to draw closer to God as she prepared to bring His Son into the world.

Elizabeth may have coached her on the symptoms yet to come, things like dizziness and weight gain. She may have told her when to expect to feel the first, fluttery kicks as the baby grew stronger in her womb. Elizabeth may have told her to expect false labor.

Joseph would not have been aware of all this, yet somehow, he knew she was pregnant. Did she tell him? Or did he notice something different about her? The Bible doesn't give us much information except that Joseph knew she was pregnant and was planning to divorce her.

Paternity was a bigger deal then than it is now and Joseph wanted to break the betrothal without exposing Mary to scandal (Deuteronomy 22:13–21). He didn't want to humiliate her by bringing her before the elders and letting them know she was pregnant.

But God had other plans. The angel appeared and told Joseph the full details. He learned how honored he was—he was the man chosen to mentor the Son of God. One of the reasons it is important for a man to have a relationship with God is because decision-making should not be based on what he feels but on the will of God. Joseph was obedient to God. He married Mary. He accepted responsibility for his ready-made family. We see other examples of Joseph's willingness to obey God.

✢ Read Matthew 2:13–23

God told Joseph to take his young family to Egypt. They had to leave their home in the middle of the night. After they had lived in Egypt for some time, God asked Joseph to relocate his family again.

Now when Herod was dead, behold, an angel of the Lord appeared in a dream to Joseph in Egypt, saying, "Arise, take the young Child and His mother, and go to the land of Israel, for those who sought the young Child's life are dead." Then he arose, took the young Child and His mother, and came into the land of Israel.

But when he heard that Archelaus was reigning over Judea instead of his father Herod, he was afraid to go there. And being warned by God in a dream, he turned aside into the region of Galilee. And he came and dwelt in a city called Nazareth, that it might be fulfilled which was spoken by the prophets, "He shall be called a Nazarene" (Mathew 2:19–23).

Like Mary, Joseph had to learn that following God isn't always easy. But he continued to be obedient. Joseph was able to obey because he trusted God.

Journal

Do you trust God?

If you answered yes, write down the reasons for your trust in Him. Write a prayer asking that you will continue to trust Him as you grow in your faith.

If your answer is no, write down all the reasons you are not able to completely trust God. Document your prayer asking Him to increase your faith and show you how to trust Him more.

A WIFE FOLLOWS HER HUSBAND

↛ Read Luke 2:2–24 & 2:39–40

No, this is not about submission again. It's about the other female curse word: obedience. To obey is to do as someone asks. It means following their instructions and complying with their rules. As we study the lives of Mary and Joseph, we see the couple traveling a lot. They went from Nazareth to Judea for the census when Mary was almost full-term. Biblestudy.org estimates the distance they traveled was about 80 miles[1].

They weren't travelling via train or in a modern sedan. This was a grueling journey through the hot dessert either on a donkey or on foot. I can only imagine how uncomfortable it must have been for Mary, yet she persevered.

To comply with the postnatal purification rites, a sacrifice was to be made in the temple 40 days after the birth of a son (Leviticus 12:1–4, 6–8). The young family would have to take their newborn baby to the temple. There they offered sacrifices to the Lord. If they had remained in Bethlehem of Judea after the delivery, the trip to Jerusalem was approximately six miles[2].

After completing this ritual, they returned home to Nazareth. I don't know about you, but I'm glad when I was pregnant I didn't have to go traipsing all over the country on a donkey. We learn from an early age that women ought to be independent and we need to stand up for ourselves. Unfortunately, that translates into a belief that men and women are in a competition. Consequently, women struggle to prove we are "as good as men."

Yes, my sister, women were created to be man's equal. We are not in competition against them. But through God's eyes, equality may not equate to women doing "men's work" or vice versa. Equality may simply mean that each person has been given a role that is of *equal value* to the role given to another person. Remember what God told Eve in the garden? "Your desire shall be for your husband, and he shall rule over you" (Genesis 3:16b).

After the Fall, the man was given the role as leader. It is the woman's job to be obedient and comply. Over the years, Mary followed her husband although she didn't know how things would work out. Being obedient to our spouse is not breaking some secret girl code. Submission and obedience are God's ideal. Is it going to be easy? No. But as God-girls, who are we going to listen to—the world or our Heavenly Father? We can't do both. We have to choose one.

Journal

What is your biggest challenge with obeying your husband?

Eleven

Who Do You Love?

She was barren. Her desire to have children would never be fulfilled. It was a good thing she was so far away from the rest of her family. She wouldn't have been able to bear having all her nieces and nephews tumble around.

For twenty years her husband prayed for them to have a child. Finally, when she had almost given up hope, it happened. She was going to have a baby.

It was a difficult pregnancy. Most of the time it felt as if there was a mini-war in her womb. When she asked the Lord why she felt that way, she found out she was having twins. She had wanted one baby; instead, she would have two. The Lord had truly blessed her.

DON'T FAVOR ONE CHILD OVER THE OTHER

↳ Read Genesis 25:20–28

The lesson of this Bible teaching is found in the verse:

And Isaac loved Esau because he ate of his game, but Rebekah loved Jacob (Genesis 25:28).

This powerful statement shows a family divided. The family dynamics had built-in enmity. These parents almost guaranteed that their children would not get along.

One thing I have learned since becoming a parent: your child will mimic your behavior. They will behave as they see you act. I'm actually of the belief they are more likely to do what they see you do rather than what you tell them to do.

Rebekah and Isaac should have told their sons they loved both of them equally. As we read their story in the Bible that is not what we see. We see a son who spends a lot of time with his mother, while the other son spends a lot of time with his father.

In Genesis 27:5–6a we see Esau referred to as "Isaac's son", whereas Jacob was "Rebekah's son".

We never see the family united. As parents, it's important for your children to recognize you and your husband as a team. Remember the whole leave and cleave thing? Husband and wife are on the same side. A house divided against itself will not stand (Matthew 12:25), and the family is no different. I've heard it said that you *have to* love one child more than the other. As the mother of one child, I don't have much to say on this topic. However, if you do favor one child over the other, none of your children should know.

Being a child comes with many challenges. They should not have to add competing for Mom and Dad's affection to the list. Each child should bask in the equal adoration of their parents. Rebekah's bias against Esau became an excuse to further her own agenda. Rebekah should have explained to Jacob his role as second-born. She should have taught him how to be content with his position in the family. Instead, she encouraged the envy he felt towards his brother. She used the prophecy at his birth to justify deceit and theft. She forgot that God's way is perfect. We only frustrate ourselves when we go contrary to His will.

Let's take an example from our Heavenly Father. God loves us. Period. No one is more valuable than the other. This applies whether we are rich, poor, or somewhere in-between. Our race doesn't matter, and neither does our gender. God doesn't have a weight or age limit. He loves us. Full stop.

Journal

What's your take: can you love each child the same? What steps can you take to ensure one child does not feel that a sibling is more loved than they are?

Connecting with your children

Here are a few tips to ensure that all of your children feel loved and favored:

1. Spend time with each child alone. Set aside a specific amount of time (the same amount for each child).

2. Choose an activity which complements the child. Use your special time together doing an activity your son or daughter enjoys.

3. Get a journal to share with each child. In it, you can put pictures from the activities you do together. Make notes about how you spent your time and the things you both enjoyed doing. This can also be a tool used to communicate with your child. Use the journal to record secret messages. It can also be used to discuss things which are embarrassing or difficult to say aloud.

4. Tell each child what you love about them. Get into the habit of complimenting them often and in each other's presence. Let each child know how much you appreciate them and what you love about them. Don't compliment one child and neglect the other.

Journal

What steps will you take to ensure there is no favoritism in your home?

If you already have children, make a list of what you love about each child. Make a list of activities tailor-made for each of them.

DON'T TRY TO HELP GOD

↳ Read Genesis 25:29–34

Rebekah had a difficult pregnancy. Though she had never been pregnant before, she knew something was wrong. When she asked, God told her she would be the mother of two nations.

The children struggled together within her; and she said, "If all is well, why am I like this?" She went to inquire of the Lord.

And the Lord said to her:
"Two nations are in your womb,
Two peoples shall be separated from your body;
One people shall be stronger than the other,
And the older shall serve the younger."

So when her days were fulfilled for her to give birth, indeed there were twins in her womb. And the first came out red. He was like a hairy garment all over; so they called his name Esau. Afterward, his brother came out, and his hand took hold of Esau's heel; so his name was called Jacob (Genesis 25:22–26).

Rebekah took a statement of fact from God as an indication that Jacob's dominance was destined. Here's the thing: God is God. Had he wanted the birthright to pass to Jacob through the natural order, Jacob would have been born first.

God knew there would be a struggle between the two for dominance. It was a struggle which began in the womb and continues today between the descendants of Jacob and Esau. God knew the younger son would prevail. Rebekah interpreted the prophecy from God as an invitation to manipulate the situation. As the mom of both boys, she should have been content for Esau to fulfill the duties and receive the blessings of the firstborn. Instead, she decided to "help" God.

The result was disastrous. Her elder son wanted to kill her beloved. To spare Jacob's life she had to send him away. She never saw him again. She spent the rest of her life living with Esau—the son she conspired to deceive. Can you imagine how uncomfortable it must have been for her to live with Esau? How guilty she must have felt knowing she had encouraged and helped Jacob steal his blessing?

DECEPTION IS AGAINST THE RULES

✣ Read Genesis 27:1–19

Rebekah listened at the door. She found out her husband was planning to bless their elder son. In an instant, she concocted a plan to deceive her husband and steal the blessing. Jacob and his mother conspired to deceive Isaac.

To appreciate the severity of their actions, we must first understand the meaning of the blessing.

For a Hebrew, the birthright and the blessing were important things. The birthright belonged to the firstborn son. Fathers acknowledged their firstborn son by giving him a double portion of what his siblings received. Deuteronomy 21:15–17 provides specific guidelines concerning the birthright.

As the older son, Esau should have taken over from his father Isaac as the priest of the family. He would have been responsible for the care of his mother and younger siblings. The blessing was in part tied to the birthright. The older son would receive the blessing from his father. Today, we disregard the importance of a blessing. We have made it a casual thing uttered to every person who sneezes. As we examine cases where a person received a blessing in the Bible, we begin to see its significance.

Let's look at one instance in Genesis 9:25–27:

> "Cursed be Canaan;
> A servant of servants
> He shall be to his brethren."
> And he said:
> "Blessed be the Lord,
> The God of Shem,
> And may Canaan be his servant.
> May God enlarge Japheth,
> And may he dwell in the tents of Shem;
> And may Canaan be his servant."

A curse and a blessing. Noah cursed the descendants of his younger son Ham but he blessed Shem and made him superior to both Ham and Japheth. Canaan (Ham's son) was to be subject to both of his older siblings. The Bible recorded the fulfillment of those blessings and curses. A man's word had power and his blessing was something desirable.

Let's go back to the account of Jacob, Esau, and Isaac.

↪ Read Genesis 27:30–41

Both Isaac and Esau were distressed because the wrong son had received the blessing.

"I have blessed him—and indeed he shall be blessed" (Genesis 27:33).

It was at this point Esau realized what he had lost. Rebekah teaches an important lesson to us wives: our husband is not the enemy. He deserves our respect, trust, and honesty.

Rebekah lost sight of what was important in her marriage. She forgot her job was to be a mother to Jacob and Esau. She had chosen to be the wife of Isaac and had a responsibility to him. At some point, she decided to put her role as a mom over her role as a wife.

My sweet friend, being a mother is a wonderful thing. We bear mini versions of ourselves and our husbands. It's our job to shepherd them through this world, but nowhere in Scripture are we told to leave and cleave to our children. Our job is to love them. To train them. To teach them what God expects so they can occupy the role God created them to fill. We are called to be intimate with our spouses. A husband and his wife should become one—united in purpose and outlook.

Read the following verses. Make note of what the Bible says about the responsibility of parents.

- Ephesians 6:4
- Deuteronomy 6:6–7
- Proverbs 22:6
- Colossians 3:21
- 2 Corinthians 12:14

Read and notate what the Bible says about being a wife.

- 1 Corinthians 7:1–40
- 1 Peter 3:1–6

- Proverbs 31:10–31
- Colossians 3:18
- Ephesians 5:22–33
- Proverbs 12:4
- Titus 2:3–5
- Genesis 2:24

Journal

What things can you start doing today to help you to embrace your calling a wife?

Twelve

The Wise Woman & Her Foolish Husband

She was a beautiful young girl who acted with intelligence and discernment. Her name meant "father's joy", "father rejoiced" or "gives joy" and she tried to give her name credence.

She was married to a descendant of Caleb - the same Caleb whom her people still talked about. At 80 years old, Caleb conquered lands and killed giants.

With such a heritage one would expect her husband to be a stalwart warrior and man of integrity.

He wasn't. He was surly, crude, and mean. He was also foolish. His name actually meant "Fool" or "Senseless".

MAKE SMART CHOICES

➔ Read 1 Samuel 25:1–13

David was on the run from Saul. He and his men hid wherever they felt safe. In 1 Samuel 25, we learn that David and his men had spent some time in the Wilderness of Paran. The account begins with a man from Maon who had business in Carmel. Maon was one of the cities which had been allotted to the tribe of Judah. Both David and Nabal were from the tribe of Judah.

We are not told how long David protected the shepherds who worked for Nabal. But it was enough time for him to have gathered information about him. David knew his name and where he lived. One day when they were shearing the sheep, David sent his men to ask Nabal for some food. We read in verse 8 that it was a feast day. David knew there would be more than enough food to share on this day. David's request was a subtle message to Nabal that he and his men deserved the food because they had served as bodyguards.

Nabal's response was, "Who is David, and who is the son of Jesse? There are many servants nowadays who break away each one from his master. Shall I then take my bread and my water and my meat that I have killed for my shearers, and give it to men when I do not know where they are from?" (1 Samuel 25:10–11)

Wasn't that rude? I imagine Nabal leaning back in his chair with a self-righteous smile on his face. He twirled a glass of wine as he spoke. It's obvious he knew who David was. Nabal knew the name of David's father. Yet, he chose not to give of his surplus. Nabal chose to disrespect the man he knew would be his future king.

Our decisions can have far-reaching effects. As wives, and children of God, we need to know how to make smart choices, because what we do affect other people. Nabal's decision almost resulted in his death and that of everyone who worked for him. Many people would have died at the hands of David's skilled men of war.

Here are a few tips on making wise decisions from Nabal's example:

1. **Evaluate the situation.** Collect as much information about the issue as you can. Analyze everything you know. Nabal had the testimony of David's young men. It would have been a simple case to find out from his staff if they were telling the truth.

2. **Determine the cost of your action.** David sent his men to ask for food. On a feast day, there would have been a lot of it already prepared. More than likely, there was more food than could have been eaten in a day. The cost to Nabal would have been negligible.

3. **Put yourself in the other person's shoes.** We can infer that Nabal was feeling smug. Because of that, he acted as if he was superior to David. Yes, it is true David was a shepherd. But there was more to his identity than "shepherd boy on the run". He was the man who had killed Goliath and restored the dignity of Israel. He was the king's son-in-law and the prince's best friend. More importantly, he was the man appointed to be Israel's—and Nabal's—future king.

Things were hard for David at the moment, he didn't need someone to lord it over him. He needed help which Nabal was capable of providing but refused to give.

4. **Think about who you are in Christ.** Make your decisions in a way which depict Christ-like behavior to the other person. Several years ago, there was a trend where Christians asked: "What Would Jesus Do?" This became a catchphrase many people used to remind themselves to pause before they acted.

As Christians, we would be wise to consider what our Savior would do on a similar occasion lest we act rashly. Think about how Jesus would respond before you do anything. It would surprise you how it tempers your actions and your tongue in most situations.

KNOW WHEN TO ACT. MOVE SWIFTLY WHEN THE TIME COMES.

↳ Read 1 Samuel 25:14–35

Did you notice how quickly Abigail gathered the food? She got two hundred loaves of bread, two skins of wine, plus five sheep already dressed. There were also five seahs of roasted grain, one hundred clusters of raisins, and two hundred cakes of figs.

Let's try to work out the timing. David's ten young men went back to the stronghold. As the young men traveled to meet David, one of Abigail's servants found her and told her what had happened. Abigail was able to collect all the food (or have her servants do it) and still managed to intercept David on the way.

David's men were warriors. They would have moved with speed after the rebuff. David and his four hundred would have moved quickly when they heard Nabal's response. These men had military experience and a bellyful of anger to drive them. We don't know how long it took in minutes, but we can infer that Abigail moved with purpose and haste.

There's one thing Abigail did not do: she did not fold her arms and say, "Well he [Nabal] got us into this mess, let him get us out." There will be times when your husband does something Nabal-like. His action may affect the whole family. It may annoy you.

You may get angry. But you have to make a choice: either you ignore his action and both of you bear the consequences. Or, you try to fix it if it's within your scope.

Don't misunderstand, not every foolish choice made by you or your husband can be resolved. Sometimes you have to face the consequences and ride it out. If you are able to resolve a situation, don't get cocky. Do what needs to be done because the two of you are partners. You committed to doing life together.

Journal

What is your typical response when your husband messes up? What can you change going forward? Find an anchor verse to summarize this new attitude. Write it in your journal and memorize it.

Know when to speak

↪ Read 1 Samuel 25:36–38

This is a hard one for most of us girls. Talking is our gift. After Abigail pacified David, she went home and found her husband feasting like a king. The man who couldn't spare a few morsels of food for soldiers in need instead lavished it on himself.

Nabal overindulged to the point of drunkenness. At that moment Abigail chose silence. She knew her words would not be well received. I like to think that during their marriage Abigail had gotten insight on how to approach her husband. She had figured out the best time to confront him.

That's a skill you'll have to master. Over the course of your marriage, you will have to learn there is a right way and a wrong way to approach your spouse. Okay, I'm going to say it: the man you dated is not always the man you married. (In much the same way the woman you were while dating is not the woman you are now.)

Hopefully, none of you went out of your way to deceive the other. But being married will reveal things you never noticed before. My husband and I dated for five years before our marriage. Our mothers were friends and we have known each other since we were children. Still, there were things which surprised me about him when we got married. There were things about me he learned after we started sharing the same space. Like Abigail, I had to learn there was a right time and place to approach him to talk about certain things.

Journal

If you want to have a serious conversation with your husband, how should you approach him? When is the best time?

If your hubby wanted to speak with you about something serious, what's the best time and way?

How does the time and place for you differ from that of your husband's?

BE HUMBLE AND GOD WILL EXALT YOU

↪ Read 1 Samuel 25:39–42

We learn from Abigail that submitting to God means He can use things intended for harm to empower us.

Nabal's story reads like a what-not-to-do:

- Don't be disrespectful.
- Don't be rude.
- Don't get too caught up with the sense of your own importance.

Abigail was the poster girl of doing things the right way. She saved the day when Nabal's harsh words almost resulted in the death of the household. She helped David recognize that his intended action was out of character and was not God's plan for him. Abigail was the personification of the Proverbs 31 woman:

Industrious.

Smart.

Able to think on her feet.

A credit to her husband (even though he didn't realize it).

Her prudence in the matter between Nabal and David brought her favor in David's eyes. After her husband's death, David asked her to be his wife. God elevated her from being the wife of a fool to the wife of a king.

It's important to note things got worse before they got better. Yes, Abigail married David. But notice what happened: he did not come to live with her in Nabal's former home. She went to live with him in a cave with six hundred men and who knows how many women and children.

She may have wondered if she had made the right decision. They had to move around a lot because, you know, a crazy king was trying to kill her new husband. She was one of three wives. She was kidnapped for a short time by the Amalekites (1 Samuel 30:1–5).

We don't know what her life was like after she married David. What we do know is when next we see her in Scripture she is the mother of David's second son. I like to think she continued to live with discernment and grace and was a treasure and joy to her husband.

Journal

How have you seen God's hand in your marriage? How has He used difficult situations for His glory?

Thirteen

What Am I Worth?

She was the elder of two daughters. Her younger sister was beautiful. She was not. Behind her back, they called her "weak eyes". Not one person bothered to look past her eyes to see who she truly was.

Maybe that's why she had agreed to her father's scheme. The new guy who was working for her father was in love with her sister. He was going to work for seven years so he could marry her. Seven years. He didn't know her father planned to trick him. She was going to pretend to be her sister. By the time he realized what had happened, it would be too late, and she would be his wife.

OUR WORTH COMES FROM GOD

↛ Read Genesis 29:28–35

Honey, you know I'm not saying it is permissible for your husband to have multiple partners. Polygamy is not God's ideal. Leah's story teaches us the importance of finding our worth in the right places. In our focus passage, Leah gives birth to four sons. Since none of her sons were twins, we guesstimate there were at least 36 months between Genesis 29 verses 28 and 35 (assuming she carried each child the full-term).

So Leah conceived and bore a son, and she called his name Reuben; for she said, "The Lord has surely looked on my affliction" (Genesis 29:32).

She named her firstborn Reuben which means: "Behold, a son![1]" It's almost as if Leah was holding up her baby up and saying, "Look, Jacob, I gave you a son."

A male child in Hebrew culture was a big deal. It meant the father would have someone to inherit whatever possessions he had. He would have someone to teach his trade to. He would have someone to help with the chores that accompanied a pastoral lifestyle. It meant when he died there would be someone to take care of his widow and any small children left behind.

But, look at what Leah said next:

"Now therefore, my husband will love me" (Genesis 29:32).

This is a woman who knew her husband did not love her. She knew he had only married her because he had been tricked. These things added to the scars which already existed on Leah's soul. Scars which told her she was not good enough or pretty enough ... that she was unworthy.

And Laban had two daughters: the name of the elder was Leah, and the name of the younger was Rachel. Leah was tender eyed; but Rachel was beautiful and well favoured (Genesis 29:16–17 KJV).

The Bible describes Leah as tender-eyed. And then, there's a but:

"But Rachel was beautiful of form and appearance."

The comparison between Leah and her younger sister had been going on their whole lives. Do you have a sister or a close relative to whom you are always compared to? Then you understand the pain Leah experienced every day of her life.

Leah was searching for love and couldn't find it. She craved her husband's affection. Each time she gave herself to him sexually, she hoped he would learn to love her. Every time she gave birth to a son, she hoped he would finally want her as much as he wanted her sister. How sad to desire someone's love when you know that person is in love with someone else.

As God would have it, Leah had a second son:

She bore another son, and said, "Because the Lord has heard that I am unloved, He has therefore given me this son also." And she called his name Simeon (Genesis 29:33).

Simeon's name means "that hears or obeys; that is heard[2]"; and look at what she said: "because God has heard that I am unloved". Can you imagine her prayers for Jacob to love her? Leah cried out to God wanting appreciation and love; wanting to be good enough. Leah craved the approval and acceptance of her husband. It never came.

By the time the third son was born, she had given up on earning Jacob's love. At this point, she would be happy if he would commit to her.

She bore a third son, and said, "Now this time my husband will become attached to me because I have borne him three sons." Therefore, his name was called Levi (Genesis 29:34).

Levi's name means "joined or attached[3]".

The original Hebrew word translated as attached is lâvâh[4]. Other interpretations are: to twine, i.e. (by implication) to unite, to remain; abide with, cleave, join (self).

Did you see it? Leah wanted her husband to cleave to her. She was longing for the intimacy which should exist between a man and his wife. She wanted what we want: a husband who cares about us.

When Leah had Judah, her fourth son, it seemed as though she had given up on trying to win Jacob's affection. She named her son "Praise[5]" with the bold declaration:

"Now I will praise the Lord" (Genesis 29:35).

My dear friend, let me reiterate: it's not your husband's job to make you happy. Joy has to come from within. This joy has to be able to sustain you through his bad moods and yours—through the days when he will ignore you because he's caught up in the pursuit of whatever it is he's chasing after. It's your inner joy that will get you through hard times. That type of joy can only come from Christ.

It is your duty to have a deep, meaningful relationship with God. Pursue your Creator with greater enthusiasm and fervor than you pursue your husband. Mankind—both male and female—was created to have intimacy with God. You do yourself a disfavor when you don't work on your relationship with God. We were created to desire a connection with Him. Many people misunderstand this craving for God and try to fill it with other things. We try food, sex, relationships, money, or drugs. This God-slot, as I like to call it, can only be filled when we have a deep relationship with our Creator.

Do you know Jesus, my friend? Do you spend time each day sitting in His presence reading and studying His Word? Do you spend time speaking to Him every day? If you don't, you will never be able to dispel the emptiness you feel inside. Like Leah, you run the risk of trying to fill your God-slot with the wrong things.

WE WERE CREATED TO GIVE PRAISE

Let's reread Genesis 29:35d:

And she conceived again and bore a son, and said, "Now I will praise the Lord." Therefore she called his name Judah.

Let us fast-forward to Genesis 49:8–12:

"Judah, you are he whom your brothers shall praise;
Your hand shall be on the neck of your enemies;
Your father's children shall bow down before you.
Judah is a lion's whelp;
From the prey, my son, you have gone up.
He bows down, he lies down as a lion;
And as a lion, who shall rouse him?
The scepter shall not depart from Judah,
Nor a lawgiver from between his feet,
Until Shiloh comes;
And to Him shall be the obedience of the people.
Binding his donkey to the vine,
And his donkey's colt to the choice vine,
He washed his garments in wine,
And his clothes in the blood of grapes.
His eyes are darker than wine,
And his teeth whiter than milk."

Judah is the ancestor of the promised Messiah (Matthew 1:3). Judah wasn't a perfect son as we read in Genesis 28. Like us, he made mistakes. But for a short time, Leah forgot to chase after Jacob's love. She chose instead to focus on praising her Creator.

Isaiah 43:1–7 reads:

> But now, this is what the Lord says—
> He who created you, Jacob,
> He who formed you, Israel:
> "Do not fear, for I have redeemed you;
> I have summoned you by name; you are mine.
> When you pass through the waters,
> I will be with you;
> And when you pass through the rivers,
> They will not sweep over you.
> When you walk through the fire,
> You will not be burned;
> The flames will not set you ablaze.
> For I am the Lord your God,
> The Holy One of Israel, your Savior;
> I give Egypt for your ransom,
> Cusha and Seba in your stead.
> Since you are precious and honored in my sight,
> And because I love you,
> I will give people in exchange for you,
> Nations in exchange for your life.
> Do not be afraid, for I am with you;
> I will bring your children from the east
> And gather you from the west.
> I will say to the north, 'Give them up!'
> And to the south, 'Do not hold them back.'
> Bring my sons from afar
> And my daughters from the ends of the earth—
> Everyone who is called by my name,

Whom I created for my glory,
Whom I formed and made."

In this short passage, we learn many things about God's relationship with Israel:

- He protected them.
- They were precious and honored in His sight.
- He loved them.
- He redeemed them.
- He gathered them to Himself.
- He created them for His glory.

Although we are not Israelites, the same principles apply to us. God loves us and created us for His glory. He called you to be a wife to your husband. You are His beloved daughter. He created you because He loved you. You were not an accident of birth. You didn't evolve from anything. You were hand-made by a Creator who loves you.

Journal

Reread Isaiah 43:1–7. What lessons can you learn about God from the passage?

Incorporating your history, personalize these verses.

How does it feel to know your Heavenly Father created you for His glory?

DON'T FORGET WHO YOU ARE

↣ Read Genesis 30:9–21

We would have hoped that after Leah gave birth to Judah, she would have realized her sole purpose was to glorify God. But, Leah is not done seeking Jacob's approval. She has not gotten over the fact that he loves Rachel and not her. The rivalry between these two sisters had grown to epic proportions.

Now Reuben went in the days of wheat harvest and found mandrakes in the field, and brought them to his mother Leah. Then Rachel said to Leah, "Please give me some of your son's mandrakes."

But she said to her, "Is it a small matter that you have taken away my husband? Would you take away my son's mandrakes also?"

And Rachel said, "Therefore he will lie with you tonight for your son's mandrakes" (Genesis 30:14–15).

On the surface, it seems they are fighting over fruit or flowers. It goes a lot deeper.

Mandrakes are a Mediterranean plant that produces blue flowers in winter. They have yellow plum-like fruit in summer. They were believed to be an aphrodisiac which cured female infertility. They were rarely found in the Padam-Aram area where Jacob and his family lived[6].

Can you imagine how excited Leah had been when Reuben brought her those mandrakes? To her, they represented a chance to make Jacob sexually attracted to her. They symbolized another chance to have a baby. Then here comes Rachel—her perfect sister, the one whom Jacob loved—asking for her precious mandrakes. Leah was not amused. She was not going to give Rachel a chance to cure her infertility and increase Jacob's desire for her.

Leah still had not learned her marriage was not about her husband. It was about her service to God. Like Leah, we sometimes forget who we are. We forget the lessons God has revealed about our identity. We forget who we belong to. We get stuck in old patterns of behavior because we can't remember the truth.

My beautiful friend, life is not about the men we marry or the number of things we acquire. Our life is about our Heavenly Father who loved us so much He created us. He wants us to love Him with everything we are—heart, mind, and soul.

Amazing as it may seem, our identity can shift based on our circumstances. It can change based on the people we surround ourselves with and the things we have. If we're not careful, we can wake up one morning and not recognize the person we've become. That's why we need to base our identity on a firm foundation who is Jesus Christ.

Colossians 2:10 tells us we are complete in Jesus. God is the only person who never changes. When we look to Him to validate us, we do so knowing the criteria will never change.

Do you think Leah ever thought she would fight with her sister over a man? Probably not. Years of being overlooked created in her a desire for something more. She hungered for love and thought she could find it with a man. She couldn't. Nothing can fill the God-slot in us except a relationship with our Creator.

Journal

How has your self-identity changed over the years? Are there any constants? Why is it important to base your identity on Someone who never changes?

WE DON'T ALWAYS GET WHAT WE WANT

↪ Read Genesis 35:16–20

What an irony. The treasured wife is dead and the woman he was forced to marry, lives on. I imagine Jacob was not amused. Did he ask God why he had to lose the woman he loved? Did he wonder if it was his fault? How did Leah feel to know the sister she had competed with was dead? Did she hope Jacob would finally love her now that the beautiful Rachel was dead?

Scripture doesn't answer any of these questions. Neither does it tell us that after Rachel's death Jacob fell in love with Leah. What we do see is this:

Now Israel loved Joseph more than all his children, because he was the son of his old age (Genesis 37:3).

First, he loved Rachel more than all his wives, and then he loved Joseph more than all his children. It seems Jacob transferred the love he had for Rachel to her firstborn son. There was never anyone who could compete with the love he felt for Rachel even after her death.

Leah, without winning Jacob's affection, became responsible for the children of her rival: "What is this dream that you have dreamed? Shall your mother and I and your brothers indeed come to bow down to the earth before you?" (Genesis 37:10)

Leah, as the primary wife, became the honorary mother of Rachel's children. Oh, the irony. Did she resent it? I like to think she accepted her role with grace; that she loved those two boys as she loved her own. I hope she mothered them for the children's sake, and not because she was seeking Jacob's approval or affection.

↯ Read Genesis 49:29–32

There is hope in Leah's story. The honor she did not receive in life, she received in death. Jacob asked to be buried beside her and not Rachel. Sometimes the reward we seek, we will not receive in our lifetime. Does that mean we give up? No. It means we press on. As God-girls, we have to learn that we don't strive for an earthly reward. We look forward to the prize we will receive when Jesus our Savior returns.

Journal

What physical reward do you find yourself struggling to gain? What advice would you give someone having a similar challenge?

Pause to Reflect

The Love Verses Check-Up

We call 1 Corinthians 13 the love chapter. Let's focus on 1 Corinthians 13:4–8 which we will use as a check-up for our marriages.

Are you patient with your husband? Do you tolerate what you perceive to be his flaws?

Are you always kind? Do you treat your partner as well as you treat the people you interact with outside your home?

Do you love your spouse only for what you can get from him? Are you jealous of your spouse? Do you envy him his abilities, job, spiritual gifts or his ... anything?

Are you flashy with your affection? In other words, do you show love to receive favor and admiration from others?

Do you do things for your husband because it benefits you?

Do your actions show love? Is the way you treat your spouse the way you want to be treated?

Are your words chosen with care and spoken with affection? Are you respectful of your partner?

Are you selfish? Is your relationship self-serving?

Are you keeping track of all the "bad" things your hubby does? Do you record every flaw, every mistake? Are you holding grudges against your spouse?

Are you happy when something negative/bad happens to your husband? Do you find joy in his missteps or misfortune?

Are you excited when something good happens to your partner? Are you happy because he is happy?

Do you give freely of your trust, hopes, and fears?

Will your love stand the test of time? Can it withstand sickness, poverty, hardships, trials, and pain?

Are you building bridges, or tearing them down?

God's intent is for our relationships to model the one between Himself and mankind. He loves us not because of anything He can get from us, but because we are His.

If we loved each other with the kind of love God intends, we would be connected to each other and intimate with God. Love needs to be the bridge that takes us out of ourselves into the other person's reality.

Prayer

Lord, I don't always love as I should. I pray You will give me a heart capable of loving as Christ did. Please give me a heart capable of selfless love. In Jesus' name. Amen.

Fourteen

For the Love of a Mother-in-Law

She was getting married. Her husband's people were from a neighboring country and the two nations were not allies.

After the wedding, she would have to spend time with her mother and her sister-in-law. Her brother-in-law had also married a Moabite woman. Would her new family hate her because of her nationality?

The media has portrayed the wife/mother-in-law relationship as antagonistic and bitter. The husband's mother is depicted as an overbearing woman who doesn't believe any woman is good enough for her son. The wife is shown as a victim who has to fight for the right to cleave to her husband.

These things do happen, though they are not the ideal. God put an example of the ideal mother/daughter-in-law relationship in the Bible. He wanted us to see this relationship through His eyes.

↷ Read Ruth 1:4–13

In this passage, we learn a few things about Naomi and her daughters-in-law:

- Orpah and Ruth had married Naomi's sons.
- Naomi had lived in Moab for approximately ten years.
- The three women cared for each other.
- Naomi was concerned about the welfare of her daughters-in-law.

↷ Read Genesis 19:36–37 & Numbers 22:1–6, 24:10

Let's have a history lesson. Moab was the son of Lot, Abraham's nephew. During the exodus from Egypt, the Israelites passed by the land of Moab. The size of their camp struck fear into the heart of King Balak so he hired Balaam the prophet to curse them. Unfortunately for Balak, things didn't go as he had intended. Instead, Balaam blessed the Israelites three times.

Because Balaam wanted the riches offered by King Balak, he taught the Moabites how to entice Israel into idolatry. The Israelites lost God's favor and twenty-four thousand Israelites died as a result. The account is found in Numbers 25.

After that incident, there was hostility between Moab and Israel. So much so God that used Moab to punish the Israelites when they worshiped idols (Judges 3:12–14). Yet, these three women showed love and compassion for each other.

My friend, there's a lot we can learn from Ruth and Naomi. Are you ready? Let's go.

LEARN ABOUT GOD

↪ Read Ruth 1:15–17

Look at the contrast between the two young women. Orpah went back to her people and her gods (verse 15), whereas Ruth begged to serve Naomi's God (verse 16).

I pray your mother-in-law is a woman who knows the Lord. If she is, you can learn from her how to walk in His ways. Naomi's life was a testimony to Ruth and Orpah. Ruth, who grew up in a culture which served many gods, learned about the one true God from her mother-in-law. Naomi's testimony was powerful enough that Ruth not only learned about Jehovah but was willing to leave her people.

Journal

Is your mother-in-law a woman of faith? What new things can you learn about God from her?

When you have daughters or sons-in-law, what do you want them to learn from you? What new habits do you need to start working on today?

CARE FOR YOUR MOTHER-IN-LAW

↣ Read Ruth 2:1–18

What would you do if you had sole responsibility for your mother-in-law? Would you care for her as a beloved member of your family? Or, would you be looking around for the nearest (and cheapest) nursing home?

Ruth volunteered to take care of Naomi and herself. She asked Naomi for permission to go and gather in the fields. It's almost as if she wanted Naomi's approval before she did anything. Maybe she didn't want to cause Naomi any embarrassment. Or, it could be she deferred to Naomi out of respect. In either case, Ruth respected and cared for her mother-in-law.

Do you respect your husband's mother? Does he respect yours? I love what Boaz said to Ruth:

"It has been fully reported to me, all that you have done for your mother-in-law since the death of your husband, and how you have left your father and your mother and the land of your birth, and have come to a people whom you did not know before. The Lord repay your work, and a full reward be given you by the Lord God of Israel, under whose wings you have come for refuge" (Ruth 2:11–12).

Did you get that? Let's put it in layman's terms:

"I've heard about all the good things you've done for your mother-in-law. You left your family and your country so you could be with her in her homeland."

Journal

What would people say about the relationship between you and your mother-in-law?

How does it differ from the relationship between Naomi and Ruth?

Later in the chapter, Ruth saved a portion of her meal for Naomi (Ruth 2:14, 18). Life would have been challenging for these two widows. Without children, they had no help to cultivate the plot of land which belonged to their husbands. Without sons, the land would have passed to the nearest relative.

If a man dies and has no son, then you shall transfer his inheritance to his daughter. And if he has no daughter, then you shall give his inheritance to his brothers. And if he has no brothers, then you shall give his inheritance to his father's brothers. And if his father has no brothers, then you shall give his inheritance to his nearest relative in his own family (Numbers 27:8).

There would have been no income and no way of getting any. The only options available were:

1) **Prostitution:** while prohibited, we know there were women who worked in this capacity. The punishment for a woman who prostituted herself was death by stoning (Leviticus 19:29, Deuteronomy 22:22).

2) **Gleaning the fields:** at Mount Sinai, God told the Israelites not to harvest the edges of their fields. This gave widows and orphans a means to provide for themselves (Leviticus 19:9–10, Deuteronomy 24:19–21).

3) **Levirate marriage:** in the event that a woman's husband died, she should be married to her husband's brother (Deuteronomy 25:5–10).

For these two godly women, prostitution was not an option. When they first returned to Bethlehem, I doubt the thought of either of them remarrying occurred to Naomi. As there is no record of Naomi working, we have to assume the two survived on whatever Ruth gathered.

LISTEN TO HER ADVICE

✧ Read Ruth 3:1–18

Okay, so I'm the first person to admit I don't always follow my mother-in-law's advice. In fact, when my husband and I were first married, I used to chafe at what I saw as interference. However, over the years I have come to realize that my mother-in-law gives sound advice. While it may not always be appropriate for the situation I'm in, I've learned to listen to what she has to say. I then evaluate it to see if the advice received is the right choice for the situation I am in.

Naomi knew a woman had no security in their society unless she married. She was, therefore, determined to find a way to take care of Ruth. Naomi did not suggest Ruth marry their kinsman-redeemer the minute they got back to town.

I don't think the idea occurred to her when they left Moab. But, when Naomi saw how attentive and caring Boaz was to Ruth, she knew her daughter-in-law would be in good hands.

When a man who had no children died, a close relative would inherit his property. This man would marry the dead man's widow. Their first child would be considered the child of the deceased. This child would, therefore, inherit the property of his mother's first husband. This close relative was known as the kinsman-redeemer. It's a little hard for us to understand this concept because nothing in our modern-day society mimics it.

It foreshadowed the role Jesus would play as the Redeemer of Israel and the Gentile nations. Israel had received a great inheritance which they lost because of their sin and disobedience. Through Jesus, the Kinsman-Redeemer, they could regain what they had lost.

Ruth could have refused to do what Naomi recommended. Imagine it: an unmarried woman going to sleep at the feet of an unmarried man at night. Can you imagine the tales the neighborhood gossip could spin?

Ruth followed Naomi's instructions because of the trust which existed between them. Ruth had proven that Naomi wanted only what was best for her. Like Ruth and Naomi, you and your mother-in-law will have to develop a relationship of trust and affection.

The relationship between a mother and son is precious. The bond goes deep and is difficult to break. If your husband has a close relationship with his mother, try not to resent it (though it's not always easy). Find ways to nurture the connection between them. At the same time, try to forge your own bond with his mother.

Here are a few ways to create a bond with your mother-in-law:

1. **Pray about your relationship.** Everything becomes possible with prayer. This is especially true if you and your mother-in-law have an acrimonious relationship. Ask God to reveal ways for you to bond

with her. Ask Him to soften her heart towards you so she can accept you as her son's wife.

2. **Pray for her.** Pray for her health, for her relationship with God, for her relationship with you and her son. Pray about the things which concern or worry her. Pray for patience or whatever skills you believe you need to be able to connect with her.

3. **Seek ways to connect.** It may surprise you to discover that you and your mother-in-law have things or traits in common. You know how they always say girls marry men who remind them of their fathers? Well, boys usually marry women who remind them of their mothers.

Don't dismiss it off-hand. You may be surprised at the similarities between you and your mother-in-law. It may be a shared sense of humor or love of romantic movies or shoes. Make a conscious decision to look for the things the two of you have in common. Make a note of them so you don't forget.

4. **Talk about your husband with her.** What better way to form a bond than to talk about the man you both love? Encourage your mother-in-law to talk about her son. You may learn some interesting things about the man you married.

Do this when your husband is present. It will give the two of them a chance to retell old stories. As you listen to their recollections, their memories become part of your story. Who knows? This may be an opportunity for you to share part of your history.

5. **Talk about your faith.** If she is a believer, ask her about her faith. Find out about her baptism or how she came to know Jesus. Tell her how you became a believer if you are one.

6. **Show an interest in her history.** Your mother-in-law is a person too. Yes, I had to say that because sometimes we forget. Ask about her childhood. I would recommend discussing this with your husband first. She may have had a difficult upbringing which she doesn't want to share. If this is the case, then your husband can let you know so you don't dig up old wounds. Pray that she will receive healing for the pain of her youth. Your husband may know some things about his mother's youth which he can share with you. Listen keenly to learn more about your hubby's mom.

7. **Look at old photo albums.** Most people have at least one album (physical or digital) with family photos. Ask about the people in the pictures. Bring an old album of yours and share some of your old photos as well.

8. **Have a girls' day or night.** What hobby do you and your mother-in-law have in common? Make a date to spend some time doing it. My mother-in-law and I share a love for romantic comedies. Having a movie marathon is one of the ways we connect.

9. **Have a spa day.** Make an appointment for the two of you to get pampered. Or have a spa day at home. Give each other facials and pedicures.

10. **Buy her a gift.** Just because. If you see something which reminds you of her or something she said she wanted, buy it for her. Let her know you saw it and thought of her.

11. **Thank her for raising the man you married.** You could do this on Mother's Day, to let her know you appreciate how she raised her son. After all, she is at least partially responsible for the way your hubby turned out, isn't she?

12. **Include her in family outings.** This is something I used to dislike. We would plan a family event and then my mother-in-law would show up because my husband had invited her. Soon, we found our balance— sometimes we invite her, other times we don't. It's important for you to form a bond with your husband and children. It is also important to connect with the members of the extended family.

Inviting your mother-in-law on family outings lets her know she is important to you. It creates connections between each member of the family. Your children learn that their grandmother is a significant part of the family.

The lessons from Naomi and Ruth apply to all extended family members. Make an effort to blend your two families into one.

Journal

How can you strengthen the bond between you and your mother-in-law?

What do you already know about her? What would you like to know? How can you pray for her?

Fifteen

A Love Like This

There was a new girl working in the fields. She was Ruth, Naomi's daughter-in-law. She was different. She was a Moabitess but it was more than that. She worked harder and longer than anyone he had working in the fields.

He heard that she had left her family to stay with her mother-in-law. After her husband and sons died, Naomi decided to return to Judah. Naomi begged Ruth to go home, but she refused. It was good to see a young woman with integrity and loyalty. Ruth was a blessing to her mother-in-law, Naomi.

As a girl who loves romance stories, I've read thousands of them over the years. I used to think the ideal relationship was a rich, debonair man who rescued a not-so-well-off young lady. The two would fall in love and live happily ever.

At the other end of the spectrum, there were stories about men who did not treat women well. They hurt them or were abusive. Both types of stories paint an unrealistic picture of relationships.

So, let's look at God's idea of how a man should treat a woman.

A MAN HAS COMPASSION FOR HIS WIFE

↪ Read Ruth 2:5–16

When Boaz met Ruth, he had no romantic inclinations towards her. He knew she was Naomi's daughter-in-law, a Moabitess. After he heard that she had politely requested permission to glean in his fields, he sought her out.

"You will listen, my daughter, will you not?" (Ruth 2:8)

He approached her with respect by referring to her as "my daughter". The original Hebrew word was bath[1] and could have been translated as the apple of the eye. Now, don't get any ideas, Naomi used the same word when she calls Ruth her daughter (Ruth 3:1).

Here's another interesting thing: bath is the same Hebrew word used in Psalm 17:3:

Keep me as the apple of the eye, hide me under the shadow of thy wings.

In Psalm 17, David begged God to regard him with the same care as he would His own eyeball. It's a bit of a graphic image but picture it for a moment. How do you protect your eyes?

If you think about it, you will realize the body is designed to protect your eyes. How many other body parts have a special covering whose sole purpose is to protect it? The internal organs come to mind because they are protected by the skeleton, tissues and the skin. But the skeleton, tissues, and skin play other roles in the body. Our eyes are so delicate and precious God created eyelids and eyelashes to protect them.

Can you imagine being the apple of someone's eye? That's how your husband should treat you and how you should treat him. Long before their marriage, Boaz regarded Ruth with respect and affection. He treated her as if she were precious.

"Do not go to glean in another field, nor go from here, but stay close by my young women. Let your eyes be on the field which they reap, and go after them. Have I not commanded the young men not to touch you? And when you are thirsty, go to the vessels and drink from what the young men have drawn" (Ruth 2:8–9).

To put it simply, Boaz said to Ruth: "Stay here where it's safe. I have ordered my young men not to harm you. When you are thirsty, drink from the water provided for the workers."

Having water to drink when you're thirsty may not seem like a big thing for us in the western world. We're used to having ready access to cold, clean water. Whole industries exist to ensure that we have water to drink whenever we want it. This was not the case for Ruth.

Naomi and Ruth had returned to Bethlehem at the beginning of the barley season (Ruth 1:22). According to Biblestudytools.com, this was sometime in March or April[2]. Harvesting barley would have been sweaty work. What a relief it must have been for Ruth to know whenever she was thirsty she could have a cooling drink of water.

How reassuring to know she could return to the same field every day. She would not have to think about going anywhere else. She knew she would be welcomed and treated kindly.

Boaz showed more kindness to Ruth. At mealtime, he offered her something to eat. We don't know much about Naomi and Ruth's life, but we can imagine that without a protector, things were hard. Maybe Ruth had planned to work all day without food until Boaz intervened.

He gave her enough food to satisfy her and Naomi. I believe Boaz chose to give her more than enough. He knew how much she cared for Naomi. Boaz knew whatever he gave her would be shared for two people—even if it was just a handful of parched grain. In this way, he showed concern for Naomi, as well as, Ruth.

HE IS GENEROUS TO HER

↳ Read Ruth 2:23, 3:6–17

Ruth followed Naomi's instructions and told Boaz he was their kinsman-redeemer. She let him know she wanted him to redeem her. But Boaz had information which Naomi did not: he was not the closest relative.

A less kind man could have said, "I'm not your closest relative" and left it there. Had he done that, Naomi and Ruth would have had to figure out who their actual kinsman-redeemer was. Then they would have to determine if he was willing to purchase the land of the dead men and marry Mahlon's widow. But Boaz did not stop there. He gave Ruth additional information:

"Now it is true that I am a close relative; however, there is a relative closer than I. Stay this night, and in the morning it shall be that if he will perform the duty of a close relative for you—good; let him do it. But if he does not want to perform the duty for you, then I will perform the duty for you, as the Lord lives! Lie down until morning" (Ruth 3:12–13).

Boaz offered to approach their relative. He would find out if the man was willing to act as kinsman-redeemer. If not, he tells her, I will redeem you and your mother-in-law. This was a big responsibility for Boaz. He would marry someone's widow, and accept the responsibility to care for someone else's mother.

His firstborn would be considered the child of a dead man. Yet, he continued to show loving concern for Ruth, "Lie down until morning" (Ruth 3:13).

The next morning, Boaz measured out six ephahs of barley. He provided enough food to last the two women for the day. An ephah is roughly 5.9 gallons or 22 liters[3]. When we calculate a liter at 2.2 pounds, we realize that Boaz had given Ruth over 48 pounds of barley. His actions were to reassure Ruth that she would be taken care of. He would do everything possible to secure her and Naomi.

He Protects Her Integrity

Let's reread Ruth 3:14:

So she lay at his feet until morning, and she arose before one could recognize another. Then he said, "Do not let it be known that the woman came to the threshing floor."

I remember reading the book of Ruth as a teenager. I couldn't understand why Naomi had told Ruth to go and visit Boaz at night. Even then I knew having a young woman visit a man at night in Bible times was not a good thing. When Ruth complied, I was puzzled. Why would she risk her reputation? What would have happened to her if someone had found out?

It had everything to do with culture. In Bible times, this was a widow's way of reminding her kinsman-redeemer of his role. It was a way to communicate to her kinsman that she was interested in being redeemed by him and was, in fact, willing to subject herself to his authority[4].

Even though Boaz understood the culture, he did not want people to have the wrong impression of Ruth's character. "Don't let anybody know you were here," he told her. He knew they had both acted with integrity, and he did not want a hint of scandal to touch her. Remember, at this point, he didn't know she would be his wife. He cautioned her to be careful so she would not expose herself to a scandal.

We live in a society where men and women indulge in casual relationships because it's "fun". Not only is it fun, but it's also their "right". Liaisons are flaunted because supposedly they make you more attractive to the opposite sex.

My friend, the devil is a liar. For years I believed the lie that casual couplings made a person more desirable. Then, I began to question it. If that was true, why do men rarely marry the women they have flings with? Why do women want to have casual relationships with the bad boy, but marry the good boy? Is it any wonder we're confused?

The devil has an agenda to destroy anything God sets as His standard. As God-girls, we have to know what God expects so that we are not confused when the enemy starts twisting the truth.

God says a woman and a man should be virtuous.

Satan says men should have multiple sexual partners and women should flaunt their sexuality.

God says male and female are to be faithful to each other.

Satan says open relationships are acceptable.

Just so we're clear, let me explain what I mean by virtue: it is behavior which proves that you have high moral standards. For God-girls, it means that we act in ways which bring glory to God. As God-girls, it is our responsibility to protect our virtue. When we marry, our husbands share that responsibility with us.

You may not have been a virgin when you got married. That doesn't mean you don't have a virtue to protect. My friend, you are treasured beyond compare. Your value to God did not depreciate because of things you did in the past. God thinks you're precious, act like it.

Journal

What are some of the things you have done which cause you to believe you are not virtuous? What are some of the things you can start doing today to protect your integrity? How does your spouse make you feel valued and virtuous?

What lessons can you teach your son or daughter about protecting their virtue?

As a note: if you're not yet married, you can have a pretty good idea of the kind of man you're dating by how well he protects your virtue. Think about the things that he asks you to do.

HE DEMONSTRATES INTEGRITY AND HONOR

✦ Read Ruth 3:18–4:12

Naomi told Ruth not to worry because she knew Boaz would not rest until the matter was resolved. She knew he would have it sorted out by the end of the day because he was a man who kept his word. Ruth 4 opens with Boaz sitting at the gates of the city. At first, it might seem like idleness until you understand how things worked then. In those days, cities had walls. There was one main gate used for entrance and exits. Life happened near the gates in much the same way it happens in a town center. If you sat at the gates long enough, you would see every person you ever wanted to see (or avoid).

Sure enough, Ruth's kinsman-redeemer came along. Boaz took the time to explain the situation to his relative. "Naomi is back, and her land needs to be redeemed. If you redeem the land you will have to marry Ruth, Mahlon's widow." At first, this man was willing to play his role. Until Boaz mentioned marriage. He backed out the agreement and gave Boaz permission to redeem the land. Could it be that the reason Boaz had not tried to redeem the land was that he had known there was another relative? Let's pretend for a second this is a love story.

Boaz noticed Ruth. He knew she was Naomi's Moabite daughter-in-law. He observed Ruth's character as she worked in his fields and cared for her mother-in-law. He was intrigued. He made some discrete inquiries about redeeming the property. He learned that he was not the nearest kinsman. There was someone else.

He knew he would be unable to do anything unless the nearer relative reneged on his responsibility. Boaz decided not to pursue it because, well, Ruth was a young girl and he was an old man. She wouldn't want to be with him anyway. He continued to act solicitously towards Ruth.

Fast-forward to the night of the barley threshing.

He woke up and there was a woman sleeping at his feet. It was Ruth. She wanted him to redeem her. He must speak with his kinsman about reclaiming the land.

The Bible does not tell us how Boaz felt about Ruth but in chapter 4, he solidified his claim on the land and Ruth before the elders. Boaz made sure everything was legal before he returned to her.

Journal

Is your husband a man of integrity? How does he show it? Are you a woman of integrity? Does it reflect in your daily interactions?

Sixteen

For Want of a Good Wife

*I*t is a well-known fact that a king must choose a wife. As the king, he could have any woman he chose. But he did not want a woman from any of the ten tribes which made up his kingdom. He decided to marry a Sidonian princess.

CHOOSE YOUR PARTNER WISELY

→ Read 1 Kings 16:29–34

The Bible calls Ahab one of the worst kings who ever lived. When the Bible says a king is good or bad, it's not analyzing the things they accomplished during their reign. Instead, it's referring to how well the king served the Lord. We read that Ahab "walked in the path of Jeroboam". He also married Jezebel the daughter of the king of Sidonia (1 Kings 16:31). The second statement emphasized the horror of the first.

Let's do a mini history lesson to see if we can figure out what it meant to walk in the path of Jeroboam.

✢ Read 1 Kings 11:26–40, 12:25–33

At the end of Solomon's reign, ten tribes from the kingdom of Israel were given to Jeroboam. This happened because Solomon had not remained faithful to God. Jeroboam was an officer in the king's army, so being chosen as the next king of Israel was a huge promotion. When Solomon found out that his servant would be his successor, he freaked out and tried to kill him.

Instead of obeying Elisha's instruction to serve Jehovah, Jeroboam turned from God. Afraid of losing his power, he banned his people from going up to Jerusalem at the appointed times. He made two golden calves. "These are your gods," he told the children of Israel, "worship them" (1 Kings 12:28).

He mimicked the worship of the true God by changing the holy feast days into days of idol worship. He installed priests to support the new religion (1 Kings 12:32–33). To be worse than this man was very bad indeed. To further compound the matter, Ahab decided to marry Jezebel, a Sidonian.

Sidonia was one of the Canaanite nations earmarked for destruction by God. We read in Joshua 13:2-6 that the Israelites should have driven these people out of the land. They did not. Instead, they allowed the Sidonians to remain and were themselves seduced into idolatry (Judges 3:1-6).

As king, Ahab should have read the book of the law:

"Also, it shall be, when he sits on the throne of his kingdom, that he shall write for himself a copy of this law in a book, from the one before the priests, the Levites. And it shall be with him, and he shall read it all the days of his life, that he may learn to fear the Lord his God and be careful to observe all the words of this law and these statutes" (Deuteronomy 17:18–19).

Ahab should have read that it was forbidden for him to marry a woman from any of the neighboring countries. God did not want His people to marry the Canaanites. He knew they would become idolatrous because of their spouses.

The choice of a life partner can have a huge impact on the course of your life. Unfortunately, this is not something we learn early enough. When I was younger, I thought I would instinctively recognize the man I was to marry. I would take one look at him and know we belonged together for the rest of our lives.

It doesn't quite work like that. Too often, we start relationships based on physical reactions. We like the way a person looks so we date them. We do not spend a lot of time exploring the psyche of the other person.

We will never know everything about a person. But, you give your marriages the best chance of survival when you spend time with your partner in different situations before you get married. This will help you to make an informed decision before you say "I do".

After marriage, take the time to learn more about your husband. What are his likes? What are his dreams? What is his vision for the life the two of you will create together? How does it complement yours?

Journal

What is one thing you wish you had known about your husband before you married him? Would it have changed your decision? How do you plan to deal with it? Pray and ask God to help you to resolve any lingering doubts.

What lessons would you want to teach your son or daughter about what to look for in a partner?

How will they be able to identify these traits in a potential spouse?

SELFISHNESS AND GREED LEAD TO RUIN

➤ Read 1 Kings 21:1–16

King Ahab was sulking because Naboth refused to sell his vineyard. Was Ahab trying to trick Naboth into giving away his vineyard? Whether Ahab would have paid for the vineyard or not is not the issue at hand. Let's find out why Naboth refused to part with his vineyard.

In Genesis 12:1–2, God called Abram to leave the land of Ur and go to a land He would show him. This was the first time God promised Abram's people a great amount of land, but it wouldn't be the last. Almost five hundred years later, the promise was fulfilled. The Israelites occupied the land of the Canaanites. Each tribe received a portion of land that was divided among its members. The amount of land given to each tribe depended on its size.

And you shall divide the land by lot as an inheritance among your families; to the larger you shall give a larger inheritance, and to the smaller you shall give a smaller inheritance; there everyone's inheritance shall be whatever falls to him by lot. You shall inherit according to the tribes of your fathers (Numbers 33:54).

It was God's will for the land to remain within the tribe forever:

So, the inheritance of the children of Israel shall not change hands from tribe to tribe, for every one of the children of Israel shall keep the inheritance of the tribe of his fathers (Numbers 36:7).

Let's look at inheritance.

The Hebrew word for inheritance is nachălâh[1]. Nachălâh also translates as something inherited, i.e. (abstractly) occupancy, or (concretely) an heirloom; generally, an estate, patrimony or portion, heritage, to inherit, inheritance, possession.

Let's look at two of those definitions: heirloom and inheritance.

An heirloom is something owned by a family member that is handed down. It can be a simple item with sentimental value or special significance to family members.

An inheritance is a possession passed on at the owner's death to an heir or person entitled to receive it. It's a legacy.

So, let me ask you the question: if you had a family heirloom would you sell it? You probably said no. If you said yes, I imagine only a dire situation (or complicated family dynamics) could make you agree to sell a precious piece of your family history.

Back to Naboth's situation: He had a fruitful vineyard. This would have been the source of provision for himself and his family. Chances are this was all his children would inherit after his death. If he gave up his vineyard, how would he take care of his family? What would happen to his descendants?

And look at the impact of Naboth's refusal on King Ahab: he sulked like a baby. He went to bed and would not eat until his wife became concerned about him. When Ahab told Jezebel what had happened, she was not amused.

"Are you the king of Israel or not?" Jezebel demanded. "Get up and eat something, and don't worry about it I'll get you Naboth's vineyard!" (1 Kings 21:7 NLT)

His greed compounded by her selfishness was a deadly combination. A man was killed so Ahab could get what he coveted. Can you imagine how Naboth felt when he heard the lies saying that he had blasphemed against God and the king? What were his thoughts as his neighbors stoned him to death? Did he have a family who depended on him? How did they survive after Ahab and Jezebel stole the family vineyard?

This extreme example illustrates the destructive effects of selfishness and greed. This may be a good time to figure out how selfish you are (let's be real, we're all selfish to some extent).

Journal

Are you someone who always wants to have their way? How often do you compromise? How willingly do you put yourself in the other person's shoes? In this account, who do you identify most with—Naboth, Ahab or Jezebel? Why?

Marriage is a partnership. What traits do you bring to your marriage? What traits does your husband bring? (Include both positive and negative ones.)

A marriage between two unprincipled persons can have destructive effects. Had Jezebel been a principled woman, she would have told Ahab that Naboth was right not to give up his vineyard. She would have reminded him that as the king of Israel he had access to much more than Naboth did.

Journal

Are you and your hubby able to offer advice and correction to each other? If you said yes, how do you foster that type of relationship?

If you said no, what needs to change? How can you create an environment where each of you is free to offer correction and advice?

Ahab and Jezebel's relationship show what can happen when a spoiled, selfish man marries an unprincipled woman. God didn't intend for our characters to get worse after we marry. He wanted the woman to be an ezer for the man. He wanted the husband to be the champion of the woman. Together, the two of them would make good decisions that left a positive and lasting impact.

This couple met their ultimate ruin: death. They had to learn that God metes out justice. It may seem slow to us, but we will reap what we sow if we do not repent (Galatians 6:7).

Journal

What steps will you take to combat your natural selfishness? What tips would you give to a young lady who is looking at you as her mentor?

Pause to Reflect

Is the Fruit of the Spirit Evident in Your Marriage?

Every Christian wants to produce good fruit because we know that the tree which does not will be cut down and thrown into the fire (Matthew 7:19). We pray for and seek evidence of the fruit of the Spirit in our lives. But, are we looking for this fruit in our marriage?

The fruit of the Spirit is love, joy, peace, longsuffering, kindness, goodness, faithfulness, gentleness, and self-control.

Do you love your partner with the kind of love Christ recommends? Is your love the kind which sees no barriers, accepts all flaws, and gives without expecting in return?

Are you happily married? Do you find joy in your spouse? Are you happy to see him at the end of the day? Are you brimming with things to share about your day? Do you crave time spent with the man God has matched you with?

Is your home a place of peace? Or, is it closer to a war zone in nature?

Does your partner feel safe, loved and wanted? Do you? Are you both able to express yourselves without fear of repercussions or an epic battle?

Are you long-suffering, that is, patient with your spouse? Or, do you have a hair-trigger temper, ready to detonate at the slightest provocation?

Do you display kindness? The simple kind that you dispense to strangers but sometimes find difficult to give at home?

Do you generate goodness? That "hmm-chocolate-cookie-is-so-good" feeling? Is your partner seeing Christ when he looks at you? Or, is he seeing someone else?

Are you faithful to your partner? Are you "drinking from your own cistern?" (That's Coote code for keeping the goodies in the partnership.) Are you careful to have emotional and physical relationships only with your husband?

Are you gentle, tender, sensitive, and caring?

Do you demonstrate self-control? Are you temperate in all your dealings? Your dress, diet, and temperament should reflect your ability to control yourself.

As Christian couples, it is important for us to bear good fruit in our marriages. Strong marriages create strong families. With enough strong families, we can change the world.

Prayer

Lord, I want to produce good fruit. Plant the seeds of the Spirit in my marriage so that I may reap the fruit. In Jesus' name. Amen.

Journal

What attributes of the fruit of the Spirit would you most like to see displayed in your marriage? Pray and ask God for ways you can begin planting those attributes today.

Seventeen

Wrong Kind of Girl

He was the quintessential bad boy. He refused to follow the rules. He made a wooden image. He built an altar to the Baals and worshipped them. He disobeyed God's command against marrying non-Israelites and wed a Sidonian princess. Pretty soon, he had the reputation of being "the baddest king of Israel". He did "more to provoke the Lord God of Israel to anger than all the kings of Israel who were before him" (1 Kings 16:33).

His wife was Bonnie to his Clyde. She did any and everything to support her husband—whether it was right or wrong. Together, they set an example of selfishness. They did more to draw their subjects into idol worship than any other royals in the history of their nation.

WATCH YOUR INFLUENCE

↠ Read 1 Kings 19:1–2, 21:5–15, 25

Jezebel is the antithesis of the Proverbs 31 woman:

- She worshiped idols.
- She was selfish.
- She arranged Naboth's death so that her husband could get his vineyard.
- She threatened the Lord's prophet, Elijah.
- She influenced her husband to do bad things.

Remember the woman we read about in 1 Peter 3:1–2? You know, the woman who lived such a godly life her non-Christian husband saw Christ through her? Jezebel was **not** that woman. Jezebel lived her life as a testimony for Satan.

Today, the name Jezebel means wicked and shameless woman. What impact do you want to have on your husband? I know what I don't want. I don't want people to say the day my husband met me was the worst day of his life. I want instead for it to be said that marrying me was the best decision he ever made.

Does that mean we will never have rough times? No. It means our marriage will reflect the growth of two persons—each of them improving over time.

Stephen Covey recommended that we "begin with the end in mind[1]". To do this, he suggested that we picture our eulogy. What do you want people to say about you? Let's make a slight alteration to that exercise:

Imagine you and your hubby have been married 50 years. Your children have planned your golden anniversary party. Your guests—children, grandchildren, former co-workers, bosses, neighbors, friends, and church family—have gathered to celebrate with you. The floor is open for persons to make toasts. What would they be saying about you if your marriage continued as it is now? What would your husband say?

Does that image differ from what you would want them to say? In your journal, write down your vision for your fiftieth anniversary.

Today is a good time to start working on the things you want to see in your marriage. Life will not work itself out like a romance novel. It takes hard work to get the marriage of your dreams.

Make a list of the things you do which drive your husband crazy. Are they character traits or habits? What can you change?

Habits can change with time, effort and faith. What we cannot accomplish through willpower becomes possible with God. Ask God to help you overcome habits which have the ability to destroy your marriage.

I know you're wondering why we didn't talk about our husband's bad habits. Okay, let's talk about them. Make a list of the things your hubby does to drive you crazy. Like the way he provokes you because he thinks you're cute when you're angry. Or, the way he puts his laundry everywhere except in the hamper. Pray about it. Ask God to help you to accept him as he is. Yes, I know you expected a different response, but it's not our job to change our husbands. It's God's job.

Your responsibility is to love, honor and serve. If we believe we can change all the quirks we no longer thank are cute, we are going to be disappointed. Or worse, we are going to become the "dripping roof" woman from Proverbs.

Journal

What do you want your husband to say about you?

What can you start doing today that will make those sentiments closer to becoming a reality?

Growing in marriage

✢ Read 1 Kings 20:41–21:4

Ahab's character wasn't much better than Jezebel's. He was sullen and childish. He served the gods of the neighboring countries and disobeyed the

Almighty God. Ahab knew who the true God was. He had seen Him stop the rain for three and a half years. He had seen God's fire consume the soaked offering on the altar at Mount Carmel. Yet, he allowed himself to be drawn deeper into idolatry under Jezebel's influence. Ahab witnessed many miracles but died without acknowledging God as Sovereign.

Let's take a closer look at Ahab reaction. In these few verses, we read that Ahab was sullen and displeased twice. In the first instance, he spared a man whom the Lord had earmarked for destruction. After disobeying God, Ahab became sulky and displeased when he heard God's judgment. The word translated as displeased is the Hebrew word zâ'êph[2], which could also mean angry. Zâ'êph only appears twice in the Hebrew Bible[2]. Both times were in reference to King Ahab's behavior.

The word we see as sullen is the Hebrew word çar[3], which could mean peevish, heavy, or sad. It appears three times in the Hebrew Bible[3]. Again, each reference concerns Ahab.

Is that you, my friend? Do you get angry and peevish when you can't have your way?

Ahab and Jezebel aren't the only ones who remain immature and selfish as they get older. Selfishness and immaturity are things we continue to struggle with until death. In a strong marriage, each person learns that they need to put the desires of their partner first. They learn to treat each other with respect and love.

Jezebel and Ahab knew how to leave and cleave, but they did it in a way which had negative effects.

God intends for us to be a blessing to others. This objective doesn't change when we become married. It intensifies. Jezebel was a woman who had no intention of changing. Long after her husband died, she continued to live a life of defiance. She showed no remorse or repentance.

↳ Read 2 Kings 9:1–13, 30–37

God had anointed Jehu future king of Israel. He was the tool God would use to destroy the descendants of Ahab. Jehu was a man on a mission. He pursued the descendants of Ahab without mercy. When he got to Jezreel, Jezebel heard about it and knew her death was near. But she would not back down.

She put on makeup and did her hair. Then she mocked Jehu:

"Is it peace Zimri, murderer of your master?" (2 Kings 9:31)

Why did she call him Zimri? She knew who Jehu was, it wasn't an accident. She called him the wrong name because she was sending a message. So, who was Zimri?

About fifty years earlier, there was a man named Elah. He ruled Israel for two years before Zimri, the commander of his army murdered him. Zimri assumed power. He murdered all the descendants of his predecessor. But Zimri didn't last long on his stolen throne. The Israelites revolted and crowned the new commander of the army Omri king. Omri, Ahab's father, led a revolt to Zimri's headquarters. When

Zimri realized the city had been taken, he killed himself by burning down his house. He had one of the shortest reigns ever: seven days.

Jehu, like Zimri, had been the commander of the king's army before his rise to prominence. Jezebel was saying to Jehu: "I'm not even going to bother to learn your name because your rule is going to be short. Someone's going to kill you and steal your kingdom, just as you killed Jehoram my son and stole his."

She knew Jehu would kill her, but she died as she had lived: defiantly. She probably hoped one of the seventy sons of Ahab would kill Jehu and reclaim the throne. Jezebel was as selfish at her death as she had been when she first became queen.

Being married is a remarkable opportunity for growth. We have a chance to learn from our spouses. As we interact with them each day, we stretch the limits of our patience, tolerance, love, mercy, and grace. We learn compassion and selflessness. We learn how to share, communicate, forgive, and a whole host of other skills. We must open ourselves to the opportunity for growth. While it is possible to mature over the length of your marriage, it's also possible to become more immature. It depends on what you focus on.

Journal

How have you grown since you said: "I do"? What areas do you need to improve on? What areas does your hubby need to improve on? (Remember we can't force him to change, but we can pray and ask God to change our reactions).

It's not your job to rule

↳ Read 1 Kings 18:41–19:2

Ahab had witnessed a miracle. Four hundred and fifty of the prophets of his god had failed to prove that Baal deserved worship. He had seen God's prophet Elijah call down fire from heaven and ignite wet wood (1 Kings 18:36—38). He had seen the rain stopped because Elijah commanded it. He had seen the rain return because of Elijah (1 Kings 17:1, 18:41).

After the sacrifice on Mount Carmel, Ahab watched Elijah, an old man, run before his carriage. Do you know any old men who can outrun a horse? Ahab was ripe for conversion. Until he went home. When he told Jezebel what he had seen, she was not impressed.

Then Jezebel sent a messenger to Elijah, saying, "So let the gods do to me, and more also if I do not make your life as the life of one of them by tomorrow about this time" (1 Kings 19:2).

Under Jezebel's influence, Ahab turned away from what could have been the greatest conversion story of the Bible. He embraced more fully a reprobate lifestyle.

Jezebel's impact on Ahab has been summed up in one sentence:

But there was no one like Ahab who sold himself to do wickedness in the sight of the Lord, because Jezebel his wife stirred him up (1 Kings 21:25).

It has been said before, but it bears repeating: the woman is not intended to be the head of the household. It's not because they are incapable—they are—but it is not God's ideal for marriage. God's perfect model for the family is Himself, husband, and then wife. He knew that unless a man looked to Him for guidance, the family would not operate as it should.

Journal

Do you let your husband lead?

As women, we tend to take over. Okay, just me then: I have a habit of taking over. I get an idea in my head of how the thing should look. Then, I tell myself no one else's vision will be as crisp as mine. As a God-girl, I am learning it is not my place to rule my household. It's my husband's. Taking a step back to allow my husband to carry out his role is a real challenge for me. Is that you, my friend?

Do you respect your husband's right to lead? Jezebel did not respect her husband as head of the household. We saw this when she mocked him for sulking over Naboth's vineyard and when she impersonated him to the people. Let's look at another account:

✢ Read 1 Kings 18:19, 19:1

The king sent a decree that Israel should assemble at Mount Carmel. Everyone was there except Jezebel. She wasn't an Israelite, but if the king tells everyone to be somewhere shouldn't that have included his wife? Jezebel did not choose to be at Mount Carmel. It was that simple. Are you a Jezebel? Do you support your husband in the things which are important to him? Do you show up where and when he needs you?

Journal

Are you a supportive wife? What can you do today to support your husband?

Instead of trying to usurp your husband's role as head of the house, focus on fulfilling your role. God created you to be an ezer, not a boss. 1 Timothy 3:11 says women should be faithful in all things. Are you consistently and diligently doing the things which are assigned to you?

OUR BEHAVIOR IMPACTS OUR CHILDREN

✢ Read 1 Kings 22:51–53

After Ahab and Jezebel's death, their son Ahaziah became king of Israel. The Bible tells us he walked in the way of his father and mother (1 Kings 22:52). When we become parents, we get a better understanding of why God called us to fellowship with him. Your children will mimic your behavior. They will speak, eat, exercise, and worship as their parents do. They won't always listen to the words we say, but they will model our behavior.

Ahaziah wasn't trained to be a king. He did not go to Kings' College and spends hours learning the art of war. There were no courses on the proper protocol for dispensing wisdom. What he had were his memories of what he had seen his parents do. They had ruled selfishly; they worshipped the Baals. He simply continued the tradition.

Do we always become our parents? No. Yet, we cannot deny that the relationship we have with them has an impact on us. The way we are nurtured has an effect on the person we become. We inherit certain genetic behaviors. My husband and I are always amazed by the similarities between our son and the members of our family. Ahaziah was his father's son.

↳ Read 2 Kings 8:25–27

Up to this point, the people of Judah and Benjamin had served Jehovah. Then Jehoram, the son of Jehosophat, began to reign. Influenced by his wife Athaliah, Ahab's daughter, Jehoram served the Baals. His son Ahaziah also turned his back on God when he became king of Judah (2 Kings 8:25–26).

Sometimes the effect we have on our children doesn't end with them. It affects the people they come in contact with. Our influence can either be a cancer that destroys everything it touches or, a healing elixir that restores. All seventy of Ahab's sons were killed.

They died because the influence of this family was so destructive God could not allow them to live.

As we read 2 Kings 10:1–11, we may wonder if God is just. Accounts like these can make us think that the God of the Old Testament was wicked and mean. The truth is that it was *because* of His love that God had to destroy the descendants of Ahab. God is merciful, but His mercy is irrevocably tied with His justice.

In 1 Kings 21:17–24, we see God's judgment being passed down. Ahab had been evil for a very long time. Yet, God appeared to him multiple times. Many miracles happened during his reign. Every appearance and miracle was an opportunity for him to repent and accept Jehovah as God.

Ahab didn't repent. He remained stubborn. Unfortunately, his children followed in his footsteps. Ahab's daughter Athaliah influenced the king of Judah into idolatry. When her son died, she thought nothing of killing her grandchildren so she could be queen (2 Kings 8:25–29, 11:1–3). Our lives affect our children's. They will either become forces for good or forces of evil. If you had ultimate control, what would you choose for your child?

Journal

What are some of your traits that were passed on to your children? If you don't have children, what traits would you rather they not inherit?

Eighteen

When Love Turns to Hate

*T*he princess was in love. He was a brave, handsome man. Everyone in the kingdom loved him. They even wrote a song in his honor. Too bad he was just a shepherd.

Imagine her delight when her father encouraged the shepherd-turned-warrior to ask for her hand.

YOU ARE VALUABLE IN GOD'S EYES

✦ Read 1 Samuel 18:20–30

For a long time, I believed that God did not respect or value women. The little I had read of the Bible showed me a God who did not name women and only put them in demeaning roles. I thought the Israelite culture belittled women. It always seemed as though the man was busy fighting to save the world, while the women sat at home and baked bread. It was a long time before I understood the truth. Women were, and are, precious in the eyes of God.

In this lesson, we will see a glimpse of how important a woman was to God and the role they played in Israel. Did I mention that I like historical romance? I enjoy reading about how things were in the past (from a modern perspective, of course). One of the tenets of historical fiction is that women needed a dowry to attract a suitable husband. Without a dowry, she had to somehow get a man with a fortune to fall in love with her. Either that or waste away in oblivion in some rural society.

One of David's reasons for not wanting to marry Saul's daughter was that he could not afford it. As a soldier from a pastoral background, his family was not wealthy. His father had eight sons and two daughters (1 Chronicles 2:15–16, 1 Samuel 17:120). So Saul asked David for the weirdest bride price ever: the foreskins of one hundred Philistine men. Before he could marry Michal, Saul's daughter, David would have to risk his life.

When some men are trying to be romantic, they claim they will cross an ocean for you and many other impossible feats. Still, do you know any men who would kill two hundred Philistines and cut off their foreskins for you?

This story, and others like it, is in the Bible for us to see how valuable women are in God's eyes. Unlike modern fiction, it was the men in ancient times that had to pay for the privilege of marriage. Your husband may not have paid a price for you, but Jesus did. He paid the ultimate price for you when He died on the cross.

Journal

If you were the heroine of a historical romance, what would be the approximate value of your dowry? What talents or skills do you have to woo a husband? How does it make you feel to know that God loved you so much He sent His Son to die for you?

What are you willing to risk for your husband?

↳ Read 1 Samuel 19:8–18

Saul wanted to kill David. He didn't care that David was the one who played the harp which soothed him (1 Samuel 16:14-23). Or, that David was one of his greatest commanders, his son's best friend or his son-in-law. What would you do if you were in Michal's shoes? I want you to reread the passage and imagine yourself as Michal. Your father tried to kill your husband, what do you do?

Me, I would be on the run with David. I don't know that I would be brave enough to handle Saul's rage when he found out his enemy had escaped. And that I had helped him. Somehow Michal discovered Saul's plan to murder David and warned him:

"If you do not save your life tonight, tomorrow you will be killed (1 Samuel 19:11)."

When her father's servants came looking for David, she told them he was sick. This gave David enough time to escape. At this point in their marriage, Michal adored David. She could have pretended not to know what was going to happen. Or, she could have told the soldiers where David was the first time they came, but she didn't. Remember the whole leave and cleave thing? That's what Michal was doing. She understood that as a wife it was her responsibility to safeguard the safety of her husband.

Who are you loyal to? How do you ensure that your hubby's safe? Not every one of us will have to physically save our husband's life, but what efforts do you take to ensure that he is well taken care of?

WATCH YOUR AFFECTIONS

→ Read 2 Samuel 3:14–16, 2 Samuel 6:16–23

Let us focus on this verse:

Now as the ark of the Lord came into the City of David, Michal, Saul's daughter, looked through a window and saw King David leaping and whirling before the Lord; and **she despised him in her heart** (2 Samuel 6:16, emphasis added).

Michal despised David. That word despise is a harsh one. It means to look at a person with contempt and disdain. It means you think they are unimportant, worthless or disgusting. The original Hebrew word is bâzâh[1] meaning to disesteem, despise, disdain, contemn, contemptible, think to scorn, vile person. How did she go from loving David enough to defy her father to despising him? We don't know how much time passed before they reunited, but at least three years and four months had passed (1 Samuel 27:7, 2 Samuel 2:1–11). Let us look at some of the things which happened in the interim:

Michal married another man

↳ Read 1 Samuel 25:44

After David had escaped, Michal was given to Palti, the son of Laish. Was this a common practice at the time? We can assume it was because the same thing happened to Samson's wife in Judges 14:20. Or, did it have a deeper meaning? Did Saul do it because he knew David would find out? Was it intended to be a trap to lure David out of hiding? We'll never know. Michal had to adapt to being another man's wife. Did she have to train herself to forget David—the man whom she had loved so much? What we can infer is that Palti had great affection for his wife.

↳ Read 2 Samuel 3:12–16

Let's imagine it for a minute:

Michal was still young when she became Palti's wife. At first, she was sullen and quiet. She had lost the love of her life, forever. There was a terrible conflict between her first husband and her father. She worried that one of them would kill the other.

Palti was a kind man. He wooed her by allowing her to mourn for her husband. He made sure she had enough to eat and the best of all the things she enjoyed. He coaxed her into conversations.

At some point during the early days of their marriage, they heard that David had married two women. Would he come for her? Did she spend days on edge waiting for him to come? He never did. Maybe she allowed herself to think of him as dead in order to go on with her life.

Palti loved her. He took care of her. She allowed herself to feel affection for him. She didn't care when David became King of Judah. He was dead to her—until the day when messengers of Ishbosheth, her brother, came to the house. Without asking how she felt about it, they took her from her second husband. She would be taken back to David.

Palti walked behind them weeping. Until Abner ordered him to return. He had no choice because he wasn't a warrior. He couldn't fight for her even though he loved her. Besides, he knew the rules: David had a legitimate right to her. He was her first husband. He was also a king. Palti turned back and went home. Michal was returned to the man who had abandoned her. The man who hadn't thought her worthy of being rescued.

Please understand that the story above is a fictional account. There is no biblical evidence to support it. But I want you to imagine Michal's pain. Twice in her short life, she had to get over the affection she felt for two different men.

Our society tells us that it is acceptable for us to indulge in many sexual relationships before, and even during, marriage. This is not God's ideal. In God's eyes, the sexual act is one of intimacy. Man and wife should have an intimate—and a permanent connection—before they have sex.

After marriage, God expects us to keep ourselves pure. We do this by committing ourselves to our partner and the relationship. We need to protect the bond which exists between man and wife. Once this tie breaks, it is difficult and sometimes impossible to repair.

Journal

Imagine yourself in Michal's shoes caught between two men, what advice would you give to her?

Is there an old relationship that still plays in your head? Is there someone to whom you compare your husband? Make two lists—one with all the attributes you wish your husband had and another with the attributes he does have. Make note of the reasons you chose to marry your husband.

Pray and thank God for the man whom you married. Pledge to focus on the good things about him when you are tempted to compare him to someone else.

David married Abigail and Ahinoam

✦ Read 1 Samuel 25:39–43

While on the run from Saul, David met Abigail. They married after the death of her husband, Nabal. David also married Ahinoam. Did the news get back home to Michal? Did she imagine her husband in the arms of these women when she herself no longer had that privilege? Is that the reason she was given to another man?

Was it because David never came for her love turned to hate? Did it bother her when David went on with his life while hers changed irrevocably?

Her father and most of her family were killed

✦ Read 1 Samuel 31:1–13

Israel was at war with the Philistines. This had been a fact of life as long as Michal had been alive. Saul's final battle against the Philistines resulted in his death. This happened while David was in an alliance with Achish, son of the king of Gath (1 Samuel 27). Michal would have probably have known that David had fled to Gath.

What she could not have known was that David secretly fought against the Philistines. Because she didn't know the full truth, she may have resented David for allying with her father's enemies. She may have believed that David had been involved in the death of her father and brothers.

Civil War in Israel

↪ Read 2 Samuel 2:8–11

Michal's brother Ishbosheth became king of Israel while David was crowned king of Judah. There was a war between Judah and Israel. In other words, her brother and husband were at war with each other. Michal would have watched with apprehension as Ishbosheth fought against David's seasoned army.

Sometime after David became king of Judah she was returned to his household. She may have felt betrayed by her brother. Ishbosheth had been responsible for taking her from her Palti and giving her to David. She would have watched as her family grew weaker while David became stronger.

↪ Read 2 Samuel 3:1

Saul's dynasty had come to an end. Most of the royals were dead, and those who weren't had gone into hiding. Michal was a woman caught between two kings. As the daughter of Saul and the wife of David, where should her loyalties lie?

Had she been materialistic, the choice would have been simple: David. As the current king of Judah and the one everyone favored, it would have been easy to defect to his side. But how could she do that without feeling disloyal to her family? How could she do that while she still loved her blood relatives and felt compassion for them?

Journal

How do you think Michal felt as she saw her family's might dwindle while David grew stronger? How would you have felt in a similar situation?

David had children

↪ Read 2 Samuel 2:2–5, 5:13–16

In these two short accounts, there were seventeen sons born to David. We know he had daughters, but we don't know how many. Despite having two husbands, there is no mention of any child being born to Michal. In fact, we read these words about her in 2 Samuel 6:23:

Therefore, Michal the daughter of Saul had no children to the day of her death.

Not only did David have seventeen sons, but he also had them with multiple women. In a society where children were praised and a woman who did not have children was considered "less than". This would have been hard for Michal. How fair was it that was David blessed with children while she remained barren?

Journal

How would you have felt in Michal's position? Are you experiencing any of the challenges that she faced? How do you feel about them?

Now that we have been immersed in the life of David and Michal, let's make the connection. This couple faced many challenges: separation, family disputes, extra-marital affairs, and outside children. This led to bitterness in Michal's heart.

Like Michal and David, we are going to experience hard times in our marriage. We are going to have things that test us more than we've ever been tested. Our ability to emerge from these trials as a stronger person has a lot to do with our mindset. Proverbs 4:23 tells us to guard our hearts because everything flows from it. I love the New Living Translation which reads:

Guard your heart above all else, for it determines the course of your life.

It's important for us as wives and God-girls to protect our hearts. If we don't, we can become bitter, old shrews whom no one wants to be around. Is that how you imagined your golden anniversary? Hosting a party no one wants to attend?

Here are three ways to guard your heart:

1. **Understand that things are not always as they seem.** If something is unclear or doesn't make

sense to you, seek clarification. Get an explanation. Don't assume. Do not try to figure it out on your own.

2. **Be conscious of the things you let into your thoughts.** What we read, watch and hear influence us. Our eyes and ears are the gateways to our hearts. Be careful what you let in through these portals. Avoid things or people with negative messages.

The Bible warns us to be vigilant because our enemy is like a roaring lion seeking persons to devour (1 Peter 5:8). Satan wants to destroy us. He will do anything to succeed. He likes nothing more than to tear families and marriages apart.

3. **Pray and pray often.** We are not able to fight Satan in our own strength. The only way to win these battles is to have God fight them for us. When our marriages test our faith, we should pray.

When things are going well, we should pray. Although easier to pray when things are going well, make it a regular practice to pray for your marriage and spouse. When you have children, you need to pray for them as well.

Journal

Make a list of the things you can start praying over your marriage today. Set up a daily schedule and start praying about them.

Nineteen

Embracing Your Identity as the Proverbs 31 Woman

Oh, come on, we couldn't have a book on marriage lessons for women and not include her.

✧ Read Proverbs 31:10–31

Who can find a virtuous and capable wife?
She is more precious than rubies.
Her husband can trust her,
and she will greatly enrich his life.
She brings him good, not harm,
all the days of her life.

She finds wool and flax
and busily spins it.
She is like a merchant's ship,
bringing her food from afar.
She gets up before dawn to prepare breakfast for her household
and plan the day's work for her servant girls.
She goes to inspect a field and buys it;
with her earnings she plants a vineyard.
She is energetic and strong,
a hard worker.
She makes sure her dealings are profitable;
her lamp burns late into the night.
Her hands are busy spinning thread,
her fingers twisting fiber.
She extends a helping hand to the poor
and opens her arms to the needy.
She has no fear of winter for her household,
for everyone has warm clothes.
She makes her own bedspreads.
She dresses in fine linen and purple gowns.
Her husband is well known at the city gates,
where he sits with the other civic leaders.
She makes belted linen garments
and sashes to sell to the merchants.
She is clothed with strength and dignity,
and she laughs without fear of the future.
When she speaks, her words are wise,
and she gives instructions with kindness.
She carefully watches everything in her household
and suffers nothing from laziness.
Her children stand and bless her.

Her husband praises her:
"There are many virtuous and capable women in the world,
but you surpass them all!"

    She used to be the woman I loved to hate. I felt as though she was a standard of perfection put in the Bible to rub my face in the fact that I will never be her. I am not getting up before the sun rises to spin yarn. I don't even know how to spin yarn. I am definitely not the one who sews every piece of clothing my family wears. Maybe you've felt that way before or you already believe you're the Proverbs 31 woman. Either way, let's talk about some of the things we have in common with her.

    The Proverbs 31 woman is a combination of Betty Homemaker and Superwoman. She seems to exist on almost no sleep, is good at investing her money, and balancing the family checkbook. She is also an excellent seamstress and designer. She never has a cross word to say to or about anyone and is always in perfectly content. She has a great sense of humor and is a joy to be around. Her home is well-tended (most likely because she has a housekeeper). She is the paragon of virtue in every way.

    Hold on girl, don't start wailing yet. We have a lot more in common with her than you think. Okay, so perhaps you can't sew a straight line either. And, maybe sometimes words come out of your mouth before you realize they were in your head, but—

    Are you a virtuous and capable woman? Do you have moral and ethical principles that you live by? Do you possess any talent or skill? Do you complete things efficiently? Do you exhibit competence in anything?

When we act in the role of an ezer to our husbands, we fulfill the criteria of a virtuous woman. Trust is an integral part of any good marriage. Can your husband trust you? Do you protect his reputation even in the eyes of those who don't know him? As wives living by the principles of 1 Peter 3:1–2, the way we speak about, and to, our husbands can have a great impact on them.

When our tongues speak life and not death or destruction we enrich the lives of our husbands. The average husband doesn't expect you to sew all his clothes. What he does expect is that they are clean and presentable.

Whether you work outside the home or not, keeping the home neat and taking care of the kids falls under the wife's jurisdiction.

"Oh, come on." you're probably screaming. "It's the 21st century."

It is. But when we burned our bras for equality, we forgot to destroy the coding in men which expect us to do these things. We also didn't destroy the coding in women that causes us to feel responsible for the home. This coding was put there by our Creator.

Oh, I'm not telling you to do it all by yourself. Your husband will—and should—help you, especially if you work outside the home. You may still have your doubts that you could be the Proverbs 31 woman, so I wanted to share a story with you:

"Mom and Dad were watching TV when Mom said, "I'm tired, and it's getting late. I think I'll go to bed." She went to the kitchen to make sandwiches for the next day's lunches, rinsed out the dessert bowls, took meat out of the freezer for supper the following evening, checked the cereal box levels, filled the sugar container, put spoons and bowls on the table and started the coffee pot for brewing the next morning. She then put some wet clothes in the dryer, put a load of clothes into the wash, ironed a shirt and sewed on a loose button. She picked up the game pieces left on the table and put the telephone book back into the drawer.

She watered the plants, emptied a wastepaper basket and hung up a towel to dry. She yawned and stretched and headed for the bedroom. She stopped by the desk, wrote a note to the teacher, counted out some cash for the school outing, and pulled a textbook out from under the chair. She signed a birthday card for a friend, addressed and stamped the envelope and wrote a quick list for the supermarket. She put both near her purse.

Mom then creamed her face, put on moisturizer, brushed and flossed her teeth and trimmed her nails. Hubby called, "I thought you were going to bed."

"I'm on my way," she said. She put some water into the dog's bowl and put the cat outside, then made sure the doors were locked. She looked in on each of the children and turned out a bedside lamp, hung up a shirt, threw some dirty socks in the laundry basket, and had a brief conversation with one child still up doing homework. In her own room, she set the alarm, laid out clothing for the next day, and straightened up the shoe rack. She added three things to her list of things to do for the next day.

About that time, the hubby turned off the TV and announced to no one in particular, "I'm going to bed." And he did[1]".

Does that sound like something you would do? Then you're her, you're the woman Lemuel's mother talked about. Embrace it, girlfriend.

Charm is deceptive, and beauty does not last; but a woman who fears the LORD will be greatly praised (Proverbs 31:30).

Notes

CHAPTER 1: MATCH MADE IN HEAVEN
1. H5828 - ezer - Strong's Hebrew Lexicon (KJV). Blue Letter Bible. https://www.blueletterbible.org//lang/lexicon/lexicon.cfm?Strongs=h5828&t=kjv

CHAPTER 2: TROUBLE IN PARADISE
1. https://biblehub.com/commentaries/genesis/3-6.htm "Was Adam with Eve when she spoke to the serpent (Genesis 3:6)?", https://www.gotquestions.org/Adam-with-Eve.html
2. H1692 - dabaq - Strong's Hebrew Lexicon (KJV). https://www.blueletterbible.org//lang/lexicon/lexicon.cfm?Strongs=h1692&t=kjv
3. Marriage & Divorce, https://www.apa.org/topics/divorce/
4. Wilkin, Jen, In His Image, 10 Ways God Calls Us to Reflect His Character Crossway (2018)
5. H7919 - sakal - Strong's Hebrew Lexicon (NKJV). https://www.blueletterbible.org//lang/lexicon/lexicon.cfm?Strongs=h7919&t=nkjv

Notes

CHAPTER 3: NO LONGER MY GIRL
1. H8669 - tĕshuwqah - Strong's Hebrew Lexicon (KJV). Blue Letter Bible. https://www.blueletterbible.org//lang/lexicon/lexicon.cfm?Strongs=H8669&t=KJV
2. H4911 - mashal - Strong's Hebrew Lexicon (KJV). https://www.blueletterbible.org//lang/lexicon/lexicon.cfm?Strongs=h4911&t=kjv.
3. Jamieson, Fausset, and Brown in A Commentary, Critical, Experimental and Practical on the Old and New Testaments
4. G5293 - hypotassō - Strong's Greek Lexicon (KJV). https://www.blueletterbible.org//lang/lexicon/lexicon.cfm?Strongs=g5293&t=kjv.

CHAPTER 4: THROUGH THICK AND THIN
1. H2555 - chamac - Strong's Hebrew Lexicon (KJV). https://www.blueletterbible.org//lang/lexicon/lexicon.cfm?Strongs=H2555&t=KJV.

CHAPTER 5: HIGH SCHOOL SWEETHEARTS
1. H3707 - ka`ac - Strong's Hebrew Lexicon (KJV)." https://www.blueletterbible.org//lang/lexicon/lexicon.cfm?Strongs=H3707&t=KJV.
2. H4785 - Marah - Strong's Hebrew Lexicon (KJV. https://www.blueletterbible.org//lang/Lexicon/Lexicon.cfm?Strongs=H4785&t=KJV.

CHAPTER 6: WHEN THE STORMS COME
1. H8538 - tummah - Strong's Hebrew Lexicon (KJV). https://www.blueletterbible.org//lang/lexicon/lexicon.cfm?Strongs=h8538&t=kjv.

CHAPTER 7: STOLEN MOMENTS
1. "10 Most Common Reasons for Divorce" https://www.marriage.com/advice/divorce/10-most-common-reasons-for-divorce/
2. Commentaries on Proverbs 31:1, BibleHub.com https://biblehub.com/commentaries/proverbs/31-1.htm

CHAPTER 8: THIS IS NOT A HOLLYWOOD MARRIAGE
1. H5139 – nâzîyr - Strong's Hebrew Lexicon (KJV). https://www.blueletterbible.org//lang/lexicon/lexicon.cfm?Strongs=h5139&t=kjv.
2. Searl, Edward Rev./ Unitarian Church of Hinsdale, IL "Traditional Wedding Vows From Various Religions" https://www.theknot.com/content/traditional-wedding-vows-from-various-religions

CHAPTER 10: LOOKS CAN BE DECEIVING
1. "The Journeys of Mary and Joseph", http://www.biblestudy.org/maps/the-journeys-of-mary-and-joseph.html
2. "The Journeys of Mary and Joseph", http://www.biblestudy.org/maps/the-journeys-of-mary-and-joseph.html

CHAPTER 13: WHAT AM I WORTH?
1. M.G. Easton M.A., D.D., Illustrated Bible Dictionary, Third Edition, published by Thomas Nelson, 1897. Public Domain, copy freely. https://www.biblestudytools.com/dictionary/reuben/
2. Hitchcock's Dictionary of Bible Names. Public Domain. Copy freely. https://www.biblestudytools.com/dictionary/simeon/
3. M.G. Easton M.A., D.D., Illustrated Bible Dictionary, Third Edition, published by Thomas Nelson, 1897. Public Domain, copy freely. https://www.biblestudytools.com/dictionary/levi/
4. H3867 - lavah - Strong's Hebrew Lexicon (KJV). https://www.blueletterbible.org//lang/lexicon/lexicon.cfm?Strongs=h3867&t=kjv
5. M.G. Easton M.A., D.D., Illustrated Bible Dictionary, Third Edition, published by Thomas Nelson, 1897. Public Domain, copy freely. https://www.biblestudytools.com/dictionary/judah/
6. Encyclopaedia Judaica, COPYRIGHT 2007 Thomson Gale https://www.encyclopedia.com/plants-and-animals/plants/plants/mandrake

CHAPTER 15: A LOVE LIKE THIS
1. H1323 - bath - Strong's Hebrew Lexicon (KJV). https://www.blueletterbible.org//lang/lexicon/lexicon.cfm?Strongs=h1323&t=kjv.
2. Barley, Bible Study Tools (blog) https://www.biblestudytools.com/dictionary/barley/
3. Bible Weights and Measures, BibleHub.com https://biblehub.com/weights-and-measures/
4. Commentaries on Ruth 3:4, BibleHub.com https://biblehub.com/commentaries/ruth/3-4.htm

CHAPTER 16: FOR WANT OF A GOOD WIFE
1. H5159 - nachalah - Strong's Hebrew Lexicon (KJV). https://www.blueletterbible.org//lang/lexicon/lexicon.cfm?Strongs=h5159&t=kjv.

CHAPTER 17: WRONG KIND OF GIRL
1. Covey, Stephen, Seven Habits of Highly Effective People DC Books; 5287th edition (1994)
2. H2198 - za`eph - Strong's Hebrew Lexicon (KJV). https://www.blueletterbible.org//lang/lexicon/lexicon.cfm?Strongs=h2198&t=kjv.
3. H5620 - car - Strong's Hebrew Lexicon (KJV). https://www.blueletterbible.org//lang/lexicon/lexicon.cfm?Strongs=h5620&t=kjv.

CHAPTER 18: WHEN LOVE TURNS TO HATE
1. H959 - bazah - Strong's Hebrew Lexicon (KJV). https://www.blueletterbible.org//lang/lexicon/lexicon.cfm?Strongs=h959&t=kjv.

CHAPTER 19: CLAIMING YOUR IDENTITY AS THE PROVERBS 31 WOMAN
1. "Find Time For Yourself" https://ed4training.com/blog/find-time-yourself

About the Author

AMINATA COOTE is a wife, mother, author, and follower of Jesus Christ. She is passionate about helping women to run their race. Read more from Aminata on her website https://www.hebrews12endurance.com/ where she encourages women to know God, know themselves and run their race.

Connect with Aminata on:
Twitter: @Heb12Endurance
Instagram: @hebrews12endurance/
Facebook: www.facebook.com/Hebrews12Endurance/

ALSO AVAILABLE
From Aminata Coote

Having a gratitude attitude is a choice. But how do we choose thankfulness when it seems as though everything that can go wrong in our lives, has gone wrong? How do we remember to be grateful when everyone else seems to have more than we do? We change our mindset.

This 21-day devotional will encourage you to find and keep your gratitude attitude. Each day looks at different things which can affect your gratitude attitude: loneliness, envy, forgetfulness and many more. A life of thankfulness in Christ will banish ingratitude so you can live your best life now.

Available on Amazon

Made in the USA
Middletown, DE
23 September 2022